PEDAGOGICAL THOUGHTS MADE FACTS

Written by:-

SAHAJ SABHARWAL

BlueRose Publishers

First Published in June 2021

ISBN: 978-93-5427-877-8

BLUEROSE PUBLISHERS

www.bluerosepublishers.com

info@bluerosepublishers.com

+91 8882 898 898

Cover Design:

Fayez Zameer

Typographic Design:

Tanya Raj Upadhyay

Distributed by: BlueRose, Amazon, Flipkart

ACKNOWLEDGMENT

My primary thanks to my dearest parents (my biggest supporters) who gave me birth on this beautiful earth and provided me an opportunity to take part in this amazing game of life. For me, they are the only Gods who really care, love and bless me everytime. My special thanks to my younger sister who helped me in a greater way at every single step of my life. An enormous thanks to all my haters and lovers, without them I couldn't grow this much. They helped me a lot to gain experience of life.

"I carry my past as an inspiration,
To provide diligent motivation"

ABOUT THE AUTHOR

PERSONALITY OF JAMMU, INDIA

NAME: Sahaj Sabharwal

Sahaj Sabharwal, a young writer and an author was born on 17th March, 2002. He lives in Jammu city, Jammu and Kashmir, India. He has completed his schooling from Delhi Public School Jammu as a Non-Medical student. Now he is a student of Aeronautical Engineering. His hobbies includes writing thoughts, listening to music, discovering new things, exploring the world, writing and singing rap songs to mention but a few. He has been awarded many awards in poetry writing at State level, National level and International level. He mostly writes motivational thoughts and on topics related to social issues for spreading awareness among the people. His writings are regularly published in many newspapers, magazines, websites, anthologies and other media platforms.

According to him,

❝ Be You

No need to update your view

On society's new view ❞

His aim in life is to invent/discover something new as a Scientist or Researcher. He wants to do something new, which is done by a few. He is an inspiration of his own. He is a successful author of the BOOK -: "Poems By Sahaj Sabharwal "

Contact-: *sahajsabharwal12345@gmail.com*
Mobile -: *+917780977469*
Instagram-: *@sahajsabharwal &*
@sahajsabharwalwriting
Facebook-: *Sahaj Sabharwal - Writer*
Twitter-: *Sahaj_Sabharwal*

TABLE OF CONTENTS

QUOTES & THOUGHTS 56

POEMS

POET, A GIFT TO THE WORLD

Writing a poetry,
Is even difficult than the work of pottery.

Making a single line to rhyme,
Requires patience, as it consumes a very long time.

Poetry is just like our inner voice,
Which contains our voice but produces no noise.

All our feelings which cannot be physically expressed,
Can be written in form of poem even when we are
relaxed or stressed.

Poem writing is one of the most important type of
literature,
Which shows a writer's observation and his nature.

All good poets have very creative minds,
Which are God gifted and someone rarely finds.

Poets live in a world full of imaginations,
But some leisured mindless fools consider poets as a
source of recreation.

In every new quote,
That a poet wrote,

Is not for someone's rote,
As it itself contain a unique deep note.

A genius thinking mind is required alone,
For writing a verse containing a peaceful tone.

Bards require just pen and page,
To share their feeling on an uncaged stage.

Poets express everything they experience fearlessly,
with the pen they hold,
As they have a brave heart which is very bold.

They are considered as the most precious gift to the
world,
Having value as pure gold,
Which is kept safely and is never sold.

– Sahaj Sabharwal

INTERNET LIFE

It's an open bet,
No one in today's world is inaccessible of the internet.

Internet has become an integral part of our life,
Without which we are not working rife.

We all are now stuck to it,
And using it whenever we walk or rest a little bit.

Mobile phone without internet connection,
Seems like a reactive (unstable) element without reaction.

Youth, middle-aged or old,
Without the internet everyone gets bored.

Under some circumstances, when internet is banned,
It shows us the mirror image where we stand,
And we can realize that how can we securely land,
Also provides us the opportunity to do something using our own brain, legs, and hands.

At that time, internet proves itself as the most valuable brand.

Internet is like that pet,
 Which convinces us to be bought in first met.
As most of our requirements are fulfilled by internet,
Without it, our life can never be all set,
Applied condition, everyone demands it's speed like supersonic jet.

Slow speed of internet really bites,
Just like irritating mosquitoes, stinging the whole night.

Life with internet always sits fit,
On proper and wise usage of it.

– Sahaj Sabharwal

A DAY OF MY LIFE TO INFINITE SKY

The frabjous sky,
Which I observed with my naked eye.
Behaves so shy,
After some time tells a lie.
And shows its clever cry
Expresses over the crops which were once so dry.

Beauty which emerges from the dew drops,
Which fits itself over the surface of the dry crops.
After that , when it stops,
Started whispering from the narrow tops.
Like that of an afraid who robs,
Every outer covering out the huts and the tinned shops.

With the entry of the sun,
News when reached the hazy day taking lots of fun.
The way I saw, the way fog taking a slow run,
The clouds welcomed the sun saying, "Sir, it's done."
"All the mist droplets killed with our gun."
Well done dear ! And thanks a ton.

I enjoyed that view,
After long time, glimpse of moon symbolizes the sun
that less time is left and minutes are few,
And today I am new.
Hope the next morning, will see you.

– Sahaj Sabharwal

STAY COOL (Poetic Rap)

Stay cool,
Don't be a fool,
Just like a mule,
Are you a dull stool?

Never be in terror loon,
Or you will see an error soon.

Do something new,
Which is done by a few.

Always be in mood,
Your attitude should never be rude,
As advised by Sahaj, my dude.

Make your own rules,
Use them like necessary tools,
And consider your opposes as big fools,
Take proper rest till your mind cools.

– Sahaj Sabharwal

FATHER

You are behind every carefully checked step of my life,
Along with my mother who is your wife.
Without your help I was not able to work rife,
And my life would resemble cutting pebble with blunt knife.

Every step of mind is under the supervision of your eyes,
While taking decisions, you are so wise.
Following your advice ,
My performance subsequently rise.

You fulfilled every requirement of mine,
Even before it was demanded my cine.
You provided me healthy, delicious meal even before you dine,
For me you have made everything fine.

I am so glad,
By God's grace, to have such a great dad.
In your presence, no one can feel sad,
And what you want from me is just a tad.

Now it's time to make you feel proud,
That's all my inner voice saying so loud.
And also in a peaceful, royal place away from huge crowd,
After all, making a confidently, relaxed rout.

– Sahaj Sabharwal

TEACHER - Our Future Maker

Giving us knowledge of something is a teacher,
Having an inbuilt experience feature.

A good teacher teaches us by heart,
And prays God for our peart.

A teacher helps us in developing our mind,
In such a way that is very kind.

A teacher teaches us tricks to achieve our goal,
And warns us to remain careful to avoid any thole.
Without the help of a teacher, we cant work rife,
And many difficulties will appear in our life.

In this vast world, they are teachers and parents only
,on whom we can rely,
They always keep on us their eye.

And we are confident that they never tell a lie,
They gives us blessings so that we can fly high.

That's why , Parents are our caretaker,
And teachers are our future maker.

– Sahaj Sabharwal

HOPE NEVER RESULTS A NOPE

Hope our eyes will never tell a lie,
And our confidence level will never die.

Hope the forests will always remain clean and green,
And the earth will enjoy this frabjous scene.

Hope our good dreams will come true,
And nobody in this planet will rue.

Hope the sun always keep shining,
And for UV Protection, ozone will always form a thick lining.

Hope everyone live in peace and harmony,
And no one will perform any illegal activity for more money.
Hope all humans will perform their assigned passionate roles,
And everyone reach their desired goals.

But most important thing is to keep scope of hope,
Which will never result a nope.

– Sahaj Sabharwal

OUR PERCEPTION IS JUST OPPOSITE

During cold winters,
We demand hot heaters.
And during hot summers,
We demand cold coolers.

During good times,
We would love to be nostalgic of those bad times.
And during bad times,
We pray to get those good times.

In normal lifestyle,
We want some twists.
And when we are lost in the complex life,

We want to live a simple life.

To be successful,
We consider struggling as the most tough so boring part
And want to succeed as soon as possible.
But when we succeed,
We consider that experience gaining part was interesting
And after succeeding, it's boring life.

When we try to accept positive vibes,
Our mind always tries to interpret as a negative thinking.
But when our mind is lost
And we consider that life is full of negativity,
Then our kind heart only helps us
With an emotional blackmail,
Full of positivity, which saves us.

– Sahaj Sabharwal

BACKBENCHERS LIFE

Backbenchers life is in another world,
Their thinking is behind it and their worthless
knowledge which is never sold.

Some of the backbenchers are so clever,
No doubt, indulged in misbehaviour, but are
mentally so strong in studies that fools can't
understand ever.

Some sit on back bench for a good view,
Of the blackboard, exceptions are a few.

Those who are weak in studies and have interest in
studying, nearly none,
Prefer sitting there to have lots of fun.

Sitting on the last seat,

For the purpose that we can easily cheat.

Is not just cheating in exam for purpose that any question we can easily beat

But it's the future of our life, burning with cheat's heat.

Being inexperienced, they think that at first they will enjoy,

Choosing a wrong path, they play with life just like a toy.

The best way is to follow parent's and teacher's advice,

They are the king of experience and for best counselling they are so wise.

– Sahaj Sabharwal

SOCIAL MEDIA VS REAL LIFE

They're the best friends on social networks,
But in real life, least talk and just busy in works.

They often pass regular time on virtual chat,
But in real life have no time for physical chat.

Mostly, they send virtual wishes and long comments online,
While real meetings yet a simple compliment is fine.

In virtual life, quite responsive to every single notification,

But in real life seems lazy and dull having no interest
in face to face conversation.

Relationship, on social media, although not so deep
But convenient and economically it's comparatively
cheap.

During online chats, people are quite confident and
so frank
But while they come face to face chat , words stuck
and mind becomes blank.

No doubt, the social media has brought in our life, an
ease,
But physical meetings are compromising, that's a real
tease.

– Sahaj Sabharwal

FESTIVAL OF RAKSHA BANDHAN

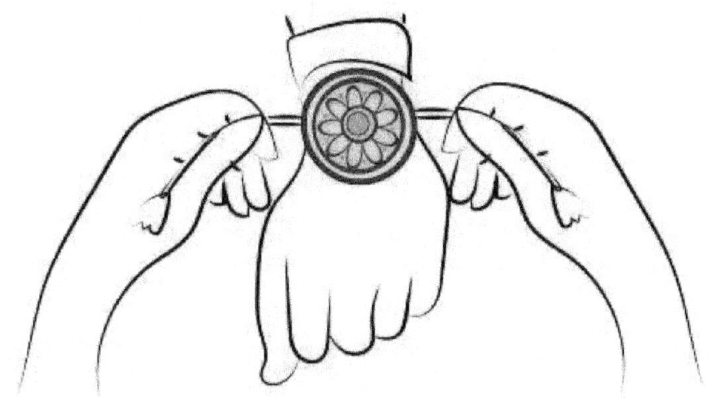

Raksha Bandhan is a religious festival of Hindu religion,

Except Hindus, people of different cultures too, celebrate it, having good vision.

A day highlighted for lots of celebrations,

Gifts are exchanged including greeting cards and handmade creations.

With love and affection, sister ties a knot to her brother,

Which denotes, the care which a brother have to do for her lovely sister under blessings of all relatives including father and mother.

The sky looks colourful with beautiful kites,

Mostly children love flying kites, from the beginning of the day till night.

Sweets, puddings and other favourite food items and prepared,

On that day, guests and relatives are specially cared.

The bond of love is increased between the siblings,

With this special meetup, everyone enjoy and refreshing memories of kidling.

Hope the festival of Raksha Bandhan fulfil all the good wishes,

Every sibling, continue this tradition and this special day, no one misses.

– Sahaj Sabharwal

RELAX WITH A CUP OF TEA

Whenever I am free,

Or want to be stress free,

It's tea,

Which works as an organic medicine for me.

Having a royal taste,

After using tea leaves, leaves an eco friendly
disposable waste.

Whenever on my desk, my cup of tea is placed,
Naturally, all wrinkles on my forehead are erased.

Pleasure within every single sip,
Takes the mind to an imaginary trip.
Holding the hot cup with a tight, side grip,
Eating crunchy biscuits after they have a deep dip.

– Sahaj Sabharwal

OTHERS ARE ALSO HUMAN BEING

Besides male and female gender,
The third category is taken as terrible blunder.

All humans including foolish and wise,
Mostly everyone do such things which indicates, their
aim is just to criticize.

Behaviour with those people,
Like they are not humans but just null or dull.

Genderqueer also have feelings and deserve respect,
If they are born on earth, they have their own aspect.

If they are not under male or female category,
That doesn't mean that they can't achieve heights and
we become their source of worry.

All we need is to be kind and change setup of our mind,

Not like that which today we understand and tomorrow again we discriminate with a heart with is blind.

– Sahaj Sabharwal

THWART NEPOTISM

An evil still alive in today's society,
Talks on this issue can no more be conveyed politely.

Nepotism is forceful building of talent in an inept person,
In this process, there is only one who run himself while other layman just hire lift for fun.

The interim benefit is availed by those who are bloody selfish,
Due to these, real capable talents, stay hidden and dismisses as their dish.

These people just work on keeping good relation,
After that comes on their exact clever need which
gives rise to great discrimination.

Living life on the shoulder of someone hardworking,
The principle they follow is just unfair profit linking.

Success without struggle is their achievement,
But really failed, bashing themselves, for their
recruitment.

There is no purpose of life,
If getting exactly what you want by favouritism,
without any efforts, without strife.
Making deserving people's life anguish, these people
regret in hell afterlife.

– Sahaj Sabharwal

CORONA VIRUS LOCKDOWN

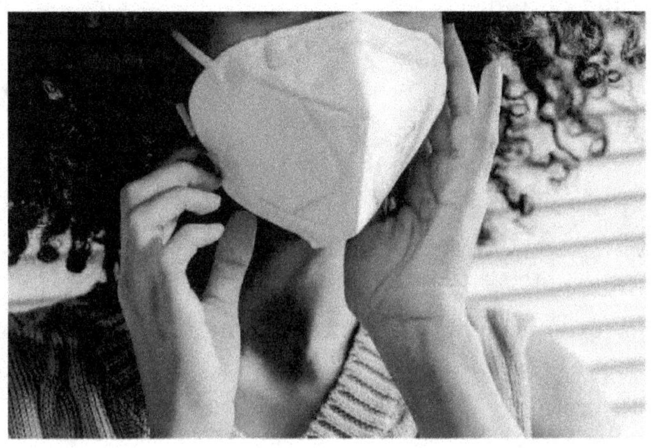

The most necessary step taken in the whole town,
To prevent Corona Virus, is the lockdown.

It is for our own good,
To stop Corona Virus, Governments of different countries took steps to the extent they could.

Covid 19 emerges as a big threat,
Having symptoms as dry cough, high fever and shortness of breath.

The best way is to self isolate,
No doubt, remaining at home only, everyone hates.
The precautionary steps, we need to concentrate,
To keep this fatal virus out of our gate.

Some people take Corona Virus as a source of laughter,
Doing nothing but being a hafter.
Making memes and jokes on it, thereafter,
But only one person, in form of God, save patients, as a doctor.

During such a long lockdown everyone gets bored,
While some careless and unlettered people being untutored,
Use unfair means to go out and all precautions, they just ignored,
Due to them only, number of Corona patients get high scored.

As no one has any alternative,
During lockdown, could not meet friend or relative.

Some people get to know their hidden talent and do something creative,
While other search vacancies and ways to get rid of this virus with respect to their nation, being native.

Following every advice of the concerned authorities and experts carefully,
Then, it is guaranteed that there will be no problem as such balefully.

– Sahaj Sabharwal

I NEVER GIVE MY PEN

I swear,
My pen, I can't share.

In fact, no one can dare
To touch my pen
When I am not there.

I am not a person with greed,
But I can't fulfill anyone's pen need.

Whether I have one or ten,
I never like to give any of them.

It's my own thought,
I am not afraid of what you think about me,
Better to have your own pen brought.

Never ask it from me, I consider it my own crime,
I will clearly deny from the next time.

– Sahaj Sabharwal

ONLY THEY ARE MINE - MY PARENTS

When everyone is there, concerned with their own lives,
Only they are here with me,
Not concerned about themselves,
But with my life only.

When everyone is against me,
Only they are with me,
And as they believe me and know me well,
Are enough against any number of people against me,
And also prove me,
Transforming all people to be in favour of me.

When everyone hate me,
And have hatred for me,
Their love is enough to heal me,

And even making them to love me.
When everyone fires on me with their weapons,
They emerges as a magical invisible shield,
Not worried about themselves,
But safe guarding me only.

When everyone break my heart,
And I am just to die,
They become my heart line,
And blessing me to live cheerful long life.

When everyone make fun of me,
Which discourages me,
They improve and motivate me,
And tell me my drawbacks,
Which everyone notices,
But enjoys scene as their source of laugh and
enjoyment.

When everyone watches the end, final result,
It only I know,
Their hard work behind me,
And the appreciation which they deserve and not me.

Who am I?
I am just a new one,
They are experienced,
But no one can imagine how will I emerge in future,
But they are indulged in me only,

Doing everything for me, more than they can.

With the grace of God,
Really they are mine,
A great salute to them for their contributions for me,
And I am blessed to be their son,
My life is fine with them only.

– Sahaj Sabharwal

DOWRY SYSTEM

The rituals of dowry,
Creates a source of worry.

In many cases it causes fights,
In which people mostly talk about their rights.

This process is just like a business related to money,
Bride is sold to her spouse and her parents provide
money or goods to him as a fee to keep her, seems so
funny.

In case the parents of the bride,
Are unable to give the demanded item, in many cases,
due of depression they suicide.

By many governments, across the globe, Dowry
system was banned,

But when carefully scanned,

Some people are still following it by illegal tricks,
which are pre-planned.

– Sahaj Sabharwal

NOWADAYS, FAIRS ARE RARE

Nowadays, we see that fairs are rare,
This is because, people prefer online shopping and
not sales in fair, no one cares.

In our childhood, fair were everywhere,
But now a days, the new generation is not interested
that much, it really scares.

Enjoyment by visiting different stalls,
Watching and enjoying the swings better than going
to malls.

Going anywhere and watching/eating different food items, it's real freedom,
But now, people consider it as a source of boredom.

Children love to go to a fair for fun,
But today, their parents think that these are inferior and has value as none.
 Confronting them and dominating a better place like closed royal shopping malls for not having stale buns,
Avoiding a fair in ground, as it is exposed to sun.

We should never forget these old traditions, cultures and practices are the backbone with which we stand,
Old is really royal but these new interests of today are not having those feelings but just a grand brand.

– Sahaj Sabharwal

TRY NOT TO LAUGH

How Sahaj does online shopping ?

1.) First of all, he search for website that will be decided by his heart.

2.) Gain brief information about the product he is buying, through online data and verifies and clears his doubts about that product from experts and relatives that are professionals. And request them, for their suggestions and guidance. He waits for few hours/days to get good suggestions.

3.) After getting all the information and verifying from everyone, the common thing that is suggested by most, get a place in the list in his mind.

4.) Checking the costs of item on different sites and choosing the least cost with best quality and checking the customer reviews/ratings.
(First preference to my heart's chosen site to buy if rate and quality are same)

5.) The product that get selected is added to cart/bag and then Sahaj takes rest for some time before proceeding further, in order to relax his mind and think that the item he selected to proceed is alright, to avoid any error or panic situation.

6.) After having rest, he verify that item again and then proceed for providing address and payments. Waits for confirmation message/email. Then 70% mission is complete.

7.) Within a few days, he get the updates for the shipping of that item and finally dispatched item.

8.) Received that product, verify the documents and the quality as researched. If found any problems in it, the product is returned or replaced by sending back to seller and keeping hope that will get expected item, if not then refund and check for another best seller for the respective product.
If the item is exact copy as expected then the mission is really complete.

– Sahaj Sabharwal

YOU ARE MINE & I AM YOURS

Real love is not just a show,
But is a mechanism that heart feelings for beloved
grows.

Caring for each other,
Not greedy about any other.

Love is not lust,
It's the matter of trust.

Never love to hate,
This problem really irritates.

Respect is the first thing,
Where she is a queen and I am a king.

Forever means till our life,
Without you my life can't complete rife.

Whether you are black, brown or white as dove,
No discrimination, if selected by my heart because its
true love.

– Sahaj Sabharwal

ALL FOR ONE, ONE FOR ALL

If the earth is a water body and humans are immense
shoals,
It is being only who controls.

The better we perform our respective assigned roles,
The easier it will be to reach desired high goals.

Living in touch of lofty height,
Neither by doing any share's fight,
Nor struggling for justice as right,
The thing is just to form a grip, which is so tight.

When an individual is lonely, it's so weak,
Just like a container full of brawn liquid but having a
leak.
Every individual is unique,
Having talent, showcasing opportunities to them
seek,
To go to the top, till peak.

When all blessed ones are together,
Like as unbreakable success ladder.
Its real strengthened wood and neither we used
tattered leather,
Nor dependent on any maimed feather.

Working in a team, not make any one fall,
Neither to enjoy playing with their talent just like ball,
Nor by cutting their legs if they are tall
Following all for one and one for all.

– *Sahaj Sabharwal*

PARENTS 👦 👧 👦 VS LIFE PARTNER 👫

Parents are always a prior relative,
Life Partner is just an alternative.

Your beloved may just try to know/understand you,
Parents already know/understand you well and will never forget you, even when you tell them to try to forget you.

Parents have an unbiased interest in you as they are your originator,
Life Partner can never take that much interest in you, parents' level is really greater.

Spouse may be your secondary love,
Parents will love you in any case, even if you start hating them, that's an exclusive love.

Parents' love is verifiable,
Life Partner's love may be variable.

A good spouse may pray for your good health to God,
But parents themselves are a form of the Almighty
Lord.

Life partner will provide you whatever you want, just
to have good impression in front of you, even if it's
not good for you,
Parents will provide you only those things which are
really good for you, irrespective of their impression in
front of you.

Parents will never demand something in return for
their love and contributions for you,
Life partner will always demand for love in return if
he/she gives love to you.

Paramour constitutes just a partner for life,
But parents themselves comprises whole life.

– *Sahaj Sabharwal*

MOONLIGHT'S ADDICTION

It's dark night,
Still you are bright.
It's night, to sleep right!
Still our eyelids fight
To be closed tight
But your beauty forces them to remain polite,
To have an uninterrupted sight.
You are creamish white,
Making dark sky and earth, look bright.
My paining neck complaining that you are upright.
Despite all you are quite quiet.
Hidden warrior as complimentary heart for many broken hearts, numbered as infinite.
Especially for you, today I write.
After the sun's departure, I shall wait for your invite,

To listen to my submitted rhyming poem that you will
recite.
But still my eyelids will try again to sleep tonight.
Please make our dissent night a decent good night.

– Sahaj Sabharwal

PEOPLE HATE MODERN POLITICS

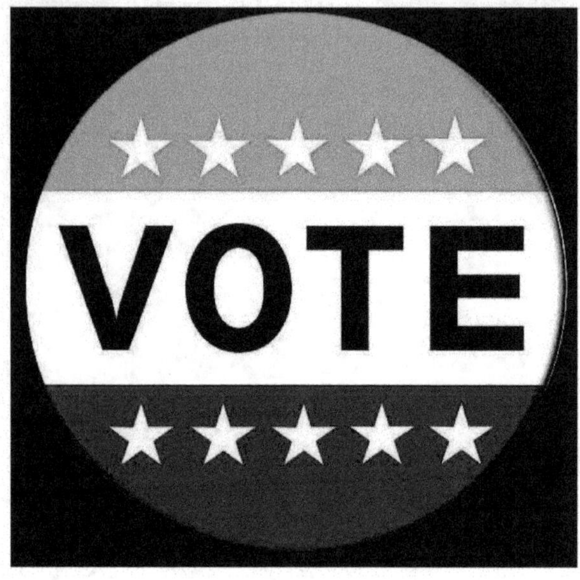

Good government is made for public betterment,
But in today's politics, politicians stand to be elected
for their own permanent employment as settlement.

As a particular party bringing its government
nationwide and their clients surrounds,
For them the whole country becomes a play ground.

Present politics is just like fighting for votes only, win
by any means and then rest for lifetime,
At such a prime position, when they neglect their
promises after elections, is not less than a crime.
Competition in an election,

Has become even more than the Joint Entrance
Examination.

Just like kids, politicians fights,
They want their own royalty which has nothing to do
with public rights.

Implementing their personal beneficial rules,
Nowadays, populace is just like slaves of these fools.

They just know how to win,
Not much concerned about their promises which
made them win.

For them, doing rally is like the game changing point,
If they're able to hypnotize the mob, guarantees a
victorious appoint.

Just for their pleasure to make name and fame,
They use people as forced players playing a rotten
political game.

Playing with the sincere votes of expectants,
Enjoying their powers as VIP of aspirants.

That's why today's populace is having a hatred for
politics,
So, don't make the politics that much lamentable as
it devastates humanity in the name of fictives.

– Sahaj Sabharwal

VAISHNO DEVI YATRA

Travelling up to the tall mountains,
On the way enjoying the view of small fountains.

Starting from the mountain's foot,
To the top, we have to walk on foot.

Moving from moderate to cold climate,
Moving together having hope with mates.

On reaching the beautiful snow top,
The view is great watching down the green crops.

Rest and travel,
Enjoying the cold water well.

Reaching the top is the real success,
Only due to Vaishno Devi, always bless.

– Sahaj Sabharwal

भारतीय प्रधानमंत्री श्री नरेन्द्र मोदी

हमारे देश के लिए हैं ये एक वरदान,

कार्य जो भी करते होते हैं प्रधान ।

सबसे प्यारा इन्हे है अपना वतन,

इनके लिए भारत है अनमोल रत्न ।

सभी नियमों का पालन करते और करवाते, वह भी बहुत
सख्त,

देश की पवित्र माटी से बना इनका रक्त ।

एकदम उचित निर्णय लेते, जब भी सही हो वक्त,

ये हैं हमारे सच्चे देश भक्त ।

सच्चाई की राह पर चलते हैं ये देशवासियों को समझते
हैं, जैसे गहने हों,

प्रेम से ये हमें पुकारते भाईओं और बहनों ।

जब भी ये करते मन की बात,

सबके दिलों को छूकर, वयक्त करते अपने जज़बात।

सब मनुष्यों से एक जैसा बर्ताव करते, चाहे वो संबंधित हों किसी भी जात यां पात से,

इसलिए हर कठिनाई को देता है देश मिलकर मात।

जो इतने वर्षों से किसी से न हो पाया,

इनहोंने आते ही कर दिखाया।

चाहे बात करें धारा 370 यां आर्टिकल 35A, इन्होंने आराम से हटाया,

गाँधी जी की राह पर चलते हुए, स्वच्छ भारत अभियान चलाया ।

आंतकवादियों को सर्जिकल स्ट्राइक कर अच्छा सबक सिखाया ,

यही नही, भारत ने अन्य देशों से मित्रता के लिए हाथ आगे बढ़ाया ।

भारत देश किसी से कम नही, पूरे विश्व को दिखाया ।

इनके कामों मे होता है शत प्रतिशत इमान,

अपने अधिक ज्ञान से ही बनते हैं ये प्रदेश की एकमात्र जान एवं शान।

इन्ही तरंह के नागरिकों के योगदान से बनता है सबसे महान,

हमारा वतन हिंदोस्तान।

जय हिन्द, जय भारत

– Sahaj Sabharwal

QUOTES & THOUGHTS

RESPECT TIME IS NOT OVER CONFIDENCE

" Today is a time when everyone play with my prospective, but time will come when respect will be my crown and no one can even be as high as my crown. In fact, people will be jealous of me."

– Sahaj Sabharwal

One can change a person physically but not thoughtfully .

– Sahaj Sabharwal

Now, people make fun of my different nature but they don't know that different people are under the talks of the people and

Become successful by doing something different from common people .

– Sahaj Sabharwal

Today my thoughts are nothing but a joke for people but with the change in time, my thoughts will be everything and people

Will be no more.

– Sahaj Sabharwal

Knowledge can neither be created nor be destroyed, it can only be increased with experience .

– Sahaj Sabharwal

Achieving success is the dream of everyone but achieved by some .

– Sahaj Sabharwal

Experience is knowledge but knowledge is not experience.

– Sahaj Sabharwal

Our mind can imagine and watch the virtual world which our eyes doesn't.

– Sahaj Sabharwal

Education is a key, which can open all ways to yay.

– Sahaj Sabharwal

Jealousy always motivates us to achieve something more .

– Sahaj Sabharwal

Studs are those whose speed get almost doubled on speed breakers .

– Sahaj Sabharwal

The fun of life is neither in the beginning nor at the end , its in the middle adventure .

– Sahaj Sabharwal

Actual happiness is not just smiling or looking happy to others, it is the state when our heart is happy. As smiling or laughing is secondary or virtual happiness.

– Sahaj Sabharwal

Respect and manners can never be shown but can be felt by the observer.

– Sahaj Sabharwal

Every human may be fake or real from outside but from the core of his heart he will be guaranteed real.

– Sahaj Sabharwal

Failure teaches us carefulness without which we can't proceed further.

– Sahaj Sabharwal

Earth gave us nothing but platform for life and we taught earth the application of the resources and made it worth living place.

– Sahaj Sabharwal

Respect is the desire of everybody's mind but is given only to those who are kind.

– Sahaj Sabharwal

Everyone aims to succeed in life but after succeeding it's actually the end of life .

– Sahaj Sabharwal

Real nature lover is that who love even the natural disasters which seems to be fatal

– Sahaj Sabharwal

A person having pen and paper is the real opportunity to show his/her creativity as he/she can bring out his talents/thoughts with them only.

– Sahaj Sabharwal

Thousands of small achievements which are the base of the big achievement are comparatively less appreciated by people as

Compared to a big achievement.

– Sahaj Sabharwal

Knowledge is that thing which never exhaust even after providing to billions.

– Sahaj Sabharwal

While taking a decision, when our heart and mind coincides, then the decision will be guaranteed fruitful .

– Sahaj Sabharwal

Understanding is better than cramming as crammed thing may or may not be in our long bit memory but understood thing remains understood

Forever.

– Sahaj Sabharwal

Handwriting never determines the type of thoughts a person have.

– Sahaj Sabharwal

If a person does not know how to live a life then it's a big opportunity for him even to get life, to learn, to explore and to remain alive.

– Sahaj Sabharwal

Getting improved day by day is better than achieving success because succeeding is a subset of improving day by day and is
Even more than to succeed.

– Sahaj Sabharwal

Great human beings are those who are fearless of death and even during the time of their death, life invites them to live her.

– Sahaj Sabharwal

Real talents are those who never show it but people in the surrounding notices and appreciate them.

– Sahaj Sabharwal

Keeping scope of hope,
Never results a nope.

– Sahaj Sabharwal

We must love all our elders because we are the future but they are the history from whom we exist.

– Sahaj Sabharwal

Dedication is wholly dependent upon our patience to be positive towards success.

– Sahaj Sabharwal

Enemies are our real best wishers as they face our angry fights and then we feel calm/relaxed to live freely and happily in

The society with other people .

– Sahaj Sabharwal

Appreciation in any field guarantees confidence level yield .

– Sahaj Sabharwal

Every human has guaranteed inner hidden talent, but to find talent is the most difficult job and trying different things hopefully to select out the best and those people are known as talented people.

– Sahaj Sabharwal

Our whole body works under the collaboration of our mind and heart and body is is valueless without them.

– Sahaj Sabharwal

Getting good marks along with good knowledge is the real aim of good education.

– Sahaj Sabharwal

Everything that looks useless show its value when it's no more .

– Sahaj Sabharwal

Heart beat is just like speedometer of a vehicle in which speed varies from time to time depending on the situation.

– Sahaj Sabharwal

Even a young child can be a good teacher for us if our hearts says we have learnt something new from him.

– Sahaj Sabharwal

A brand new notebook has no value until we write/create something and make it valuable.

– Sahaj Sabharwal

Respect is like a bullet of gun which travels with us in a long run .

– Sahaj Sabharwal

Hard work does not result in desired position always but it always teaches us valuable lesson, which if we take seriously, is a shortcut to the
Required position.

– Sahaj Sabharwal

To live in peace and harmony,
The most important tool is to strictly follow every rule.

– Sahaj Sabharwal

When we have any terror,
It will always results an error.

– Sahaj Sabharwal

Giving something physically aims at getting something in exchange but giving something non materialistic aims but person may or may not get something in return.

– Sahaj Sabharwal

We must consider even a single problem light because at last these little problems reaches greater heights and hence tightly
Bites.

– Sahaj Sabharwal

Taking every useful thing seriously is necessary for being dedicated.

– Sahaj Sabharwal

Real love is that love which is never shown, even hidden, but felt by the love.

– Sahaj Sabharwal

"Mostly when people having less time are not able to understand a write up with deep thoughts with respect to an author, they consider it boring or not good "

– Sahaj Sabharwal

"Every harmful attack of an enemy, brings with it a tendency to learn something new which can be enhanced further as a try to be used as a shield to defend in a disastrous smash reply "

– Sahaj Sabharwal

"When high level person falls to lower level then the person who is already at lower level has big opportunity to rise up to a higher level, out of motivation with a progress scope "

– Sahaj Sabharwal

SPECTACLES

People with a bad vision are infamous as they use spectacles.

But as their vision is not good are dependent on spectacles only for clear view and their natural eye is protected from dust, dirt, pollution and even fatal virus to some extent as compared to those whose vision are good (6/6)

As life is more important than good vision.

Bad vision people are blessed to have such a plus point security.

So never be discouraged, if you have a disability, you will definitely have an advantage too, which good ability common or ideal person might not have.

– Sahaj Sabharwal

REAL THOUGHTS

Real thoughts are those,
Which once vanished never come again.

– Sahaj Sabharwal

MY SERIOUS TALKS

Relatives: Sahaj, why you take every single precaution to prevent corona virus, so seriously ?

Me: because i don't take risks as precautions are better than to cure.

Relatives: we also take precautions but not seriously as you take, we believe that if death will come we noone can save us.

Me: you must also follow precautions seriously as i do not want that only i stay alive and you all not with me, then who will make fun of my seriousness ?

Relatives: Ohhhh

– Sahaj Sabharwal

" If you feel glad that you understand me well,
Sorry you are in big misconception as you take me
simple as wrong "

– Sahaj Sabharwal

My coffee
A dark coffee rich in caffeine,
Design of white, heart shaped cream,
Touching the brim, making sassy scene,
Induce enthusiasm in me, is what i mean.

– Sahaj Sabharwal

Old is really royal,
New is never loyal.

– Sahaj Sabharwal

Smart minded children don't feel upset even when
teacher slaps them tightly as they think that if teacher
slaps their face, then their face too hits the teacher's
hand with equal force following newton's 3rd law.

– Sahaj Sabharwal

Bad attitude
Really rude
Depends on mood
Can make you its food
It is not good, you conclude

– Sahaj Sabharwal

The best way to impress,
Independent of how you dress.
First thing is to have no stress,
Just be confident, no matter what you express.
God bless,
You will definitely hear a rare yes.

– Sahaj Sabharwal

Copy and paste without taste,
Is noting but your life's savvy is waste.

– Sahaj Sabharwal

For those who are middle or average,
No fortuitous benefit granted, but savage.
The advantage is for high wage and low wage,
What remarkably shown is just a virtual image.
But middle class have tendency to bear every damage.

– Sahaj Sabharwal

" When you are not a pro,
Then only you have the opportunity to totes grow "

– Sahaj Sabharwal

The greater the level in a particular field,
The greater will the struggle to keep it up as high yield.
- Sahaj Sabharwal

When you have nothing then life really starts,
When you have everything then life virtually stops.
- Sahaj Sabharwal

Never wait for others to motivate you,
Be an inbuilt motivation within you.
- Sahaj Sabharwal

Talent
If you are not rare
Then i am not here
To pay fare
Take care

- Sahaj Sabharwal

Nowadays,
"Death has become rebirth of humanity"
- Sahaj Sabharwal

If you show off in front of someone will not bring
fame but blame,
While showing yourself your reality is key to the
winner's game.

– Sahaj Sabharwal

Nepotism
Success without struggle,
Triumphant in front of world,
But a big failure, bashing themselves as soliloquy.

– Sahaj Sabharwal

Never hate those who irritate,
As they are just helping you boost your capability even
in hard situations.

– Sahaj Sabharwal

Use attitude in good works
If your passion is just to show your attitude as proud,
Then it's an opportunity for you to bring back sense
of humanity in busting crowd.
Then you really deserve to be proud.

– Sahaj Sabharwal

" Forceful building of talent in an inept person is the real characteristic of nepotism "

– Sahaj Sabharwal

" It is today only on which result depends, will only make yesterday as everyday "

– Sahaj Sabharwal

A self motivated person work sprightly on negative insults,
To get positive results.

– Sahaj Sabharwal

When people consider me fool watching just my activities, i feel so happy as i am so intelligent in making people fool easily by my physical appearance ! Lol !

– Sahaj Sabharwal

We think that if we are doing everything in a correct way, then we will definitely achieve success but the truth is that if someone is doing wrong on our path to success, then it can deviate us from our path if we don't have tendency to defend in a right way

– Sahaj Sabharwal

Correct technique dominates availability
Bright light on a dark way helps in a clear sight,
But someone on a dark way, throwing bright light on
our eyes, can make us blind.

– Sahaj Sabharwal

Only high level and low level are noticed,
Either praises to high level or criticizes to low level.
Intermediate level is worthless.

– Sahaj Sabharwal

We all are advised not to eavesdrop
No doubt, it helps in suspending suspense
But it creates avoidable tensions and pressure over
brain.

– Sahaj Sabharwal

Confidence is more important,
No matter whatever you speak "

– Sahaj Sabharwal

Ego supports attitude to constrain a person to be
selfish

– Sahaj Sabharwal

Every person has different god gifted skills,
No need to copy any other person by taking phoney pills

– Sahaj Sabharwal

A human being works until he is not satisfied,
The day he will be fully satisfied, the motive of his life will be completed.

– Sahaj Sabharwal

Greed is an unsatisfactory human need,
Which requires no feed to breed

– Sahaj Sabharwal

Don't worry about what someone thinks about you.
Care about what you think about you.

– Sahaj Sabharwal

Deed is just a bell,
Which signifies you are about to enter heaven or hell

– Sahaj Sabharwal

Triumph in any field,
Is in the hand of a passionate stakeholder.

– Sahaj Sabharwal

That love is never real in which a beautiful girl like dove,
When loses her beauty and not looking like before,
The lover stops loving her.

– Sahaj Sabharwal

A person who changes himself on the suggestion or belief of someone is fake because remake is always fake.

– Sahaj Sabharwal

Pressure creates diamond,
But pressure over diamond vapourizes it, as the temperature increases and it gets heated up.
So, excess of anything can even blame you for the loss of valuable presence.

– Sahaj Sabharwal

Writer is a brave mind fighter,
Having a pen full of heavy thoughts,
But is still lighter

– Sahaj Sabharwal

The time when ego takes the place of self-esteem,
It is an indication that you are on the path of catastrophe

– Sahaj Sabharwal

If you have done a mistake then don't feel upset,
But you should be glad.
As the lesson you learnt from it can help prevent further mistake in future.

– Sahaj Sabharwal

We mustn't keep searching for opportunities,
But for our abilities and potential.
Because whenever an opportunity seeks us,
Then, we will be capable to command on the strength of our skills and will not lose the opportunity.

– Sahaj Sabharwal

An upright person will never implore someone for getting a like,
But will like those who dislike him, when he never deserve a like.

– Sahaj Sabharwal

Being simple is also a style
If you are not simple,
It's your choice.
But you are in that condition,
In which you have to be confined.
Which is not compulsory,
Just your wish.

– Sahaj Sabharwal

Never copy someone you rely,
Just take an inspiration and apply

– Sahaj Sabharwal

2020
Lift in time is a shift,
Not less than a gift

– Sahaj Sabharwal

You are on the correct line,

If you compare your qualities neither with others nor with mine.

But compare your own individual qualities which will help you feel that some of your qualities are also fine.

It will create your another level and will induce scope of hope which your heart and mind never decline.

You will get correct definition which you define.

– Sahaj Sabharwal

Are people ghost ?

Why to fear of what people will think or say !

You must do whatever you want and these people should fear of your action.

– Sahaj Sabharwal

The main difference between

Success
It's easy to take up risk,
But difficult to give up.
&
Failure
It's difficult to take up risk,
But easy to give up.

– Sahaj Sabharwal

Struggle, sacrifice & stress are the three s's on the path
to success

– Sahaj Sabharwal

What you deserve,
Is what you serve.
For reaction you observe,
For continuity you preserve.

– Sahaj Sabharwal

Every single thing counts,
Only if you have a container to collect and check
amounts.

– Sahaj Sabharwal

Nowadays,
Stingy and greedy are the new whip-smart

– Sahaj Sabharwal

Show what you feel,
Not what others make you feel.

– Sahaj Sabharwal

Nobody's mind is weak,
What matters to triumph are your thoughts, they must be unique

– Sahaj Sabharwal

When i speak,
I might be shy
To express, words can be a lie.

When i write
I give my first and last try,
And no one can stop me to fly high in the sky.

– Sahaj Sabharwal

What hurts the most
Is not the people,
But their thinking.

– Sahaj Sabharwal

Breaking a new record towards your goal everyday,
Is the real proof of success.

– Sahaj Sabharwal

If you are a creative writer,
Then, express your sight.
Not that erratic people will make you write.
Because you are a creative writer, not them.

– Sahaj Sabharwal

Reading me is like -:
Throwing your brain away from your body
&
Learning to respect and follow your heart.

– Sahaj Sabharwal

The greater the problems in life,
The interesting will be the story of life

– Sahaj Sabharwal

Nowadays,
Motivators are more
Motivated are less.

– Sahaj Sabharwal

Society said
Respect and save women and provide them safe environment.

Girl replied
But why they have forgotten about men,
Now a days, men are disrespected too and they are also not safe. Talk about them too.
Respect and save men and provide them safe environment too.

– Sahaj Sabharwal

Take even useless things as useful
Because when nothing happens,
Then, useless things prove to be a game changer.

– Sahaj Sabharwal

No one is perfect,
But those who did it,
Their destination is always erect.

– Sahaj Sabharwal

Be creative
Never invest to be talented.
If you are really talented,
Then, investors will seek and invest on you.

– Sahaj Sabharwal

Try to be creative,
Not just envious of your creative relative.

– Sahaj Sabharwal

Failure isn't not getting success,
Failure is not getting experience.

– Sahaj Sabharwal

Try to improve,
Then there will be no need to prove

– Sahaj Sabharwal

Be rare,
Otherwise no one will care

– Sahaj Sabharwal

Night is proof,
That darkness is a part of everyone's life

– Sahaj Sabharwal

It's better to forgive,
If you believe in deeds.

– Sahaj Sabharwal

An inexpert will never understand the behind camera sweat guts out but will appreciate the outcome movie even without thinking

– Sahaj Sabharwal

Be that much capable that
You decide to take luck with you on the way to success, not luck

– Sahaj Sabharwal

It's better to grow and go up slowly but carefully,
To reach a greater height
Rather than to step down from the respective position of greediness

– Sahaj Sabharwal

If you made a mistake,
Don't worry, you did the right thing.
Because if someone loses, then only one can win.
If you have lost, it helps someone to win.
Continuous progress of one can be stressful and may lead to loss of the other.
Helping someone is sometimes a good work.

– Sahaj Sabharwal

Forget yesterday
Take care of today
To have a better next day

– Sahaj Sabharwal

Some try to be good
Others try not to be bad
I try to be unique against illusion

– Sahaj Sabharwal

Every attack of an opponent is an opportunity for you

1.) Depends upon you that which step you take on your turn
2.) You can upraise new tactics and learn
3.) Or with the performance of opponent just surrender and burn

– Sahaj Sabharwal

Negativity is a part of life.
We can't stop it.
But we can try to dominate positivity
So that negativity can be ignored

– Sahaj Sabharwal

I am the owner of my own style,
Not a fake one, that your compliments will rule
and change my profile

– Sahaj Sabharwal

Dear mate,
Don't hate,
If you can't relate.

– Sahaj Sabharwal

Support those people you think are right,
But no one supports them

– Sahaj Sabharwal

Don't just follow and support a trend or meme
Try to be a trend,
Almost everyone have this dream
Contribute to you too

– Sahaj Sabharwal

Never wait for opportunities
Wait for being more proficient
Because if by chance opportunity arrives you before
you are skilled,
Then you will lose it.

– Sahaj Sabharwal

Love is not a force,
But it is a source,
Which provides us an important course,
In which the key point is to learn to admire to enforce.

– Sahaj Sabharwal

Aim of fair love with care is -:
To feel, understand and heal every pain
To become same blood in a single vein
To remain together forever, whether its sunny or rains
To follow each others heart and forget brain

– Sahaj Sabharwal

Manners provides mind's attraction
Actuality provides heart's relaxation

– Sahaj Sabharwal

Our mind can't delete
Those thoughts which our mind continuously repeats

– Sahaj Sabharwal

Work will be done in the best way,
When the opinion of both mind & heart coincides

– Sahaj Sabharwal

Creativity is not formality
It's reality

– Sahaj Sabharwal

Organic way to promote
Is to support
As a vote

– Sahaj Sabharwal

Be you
No need to update your view
On society's new view

– Sahaj Sabharwal

Mental stress results in distress
Due to rift between heart and mind
That's why be your own motivation

– Sahaj Sabharwal

Success and failure are just tags, for those who even
try,
Real failure deserves those, who lags behind and cry
but can't dare to try.

– Sahaj Sabharwal

Love, when it arrives,
Looks like I won the game of love

Love when it leaves,
Looks like love won the game of mine.

– Sahaj Sabharwal

Fair people are rare
Because no one cares
Demotivated reality disappears

– Sahaj Sabharwal

Living in my own way,
Being unique, fearless & independent
As i am the owner of my life.

– Sahaj Sabharwal

Experience
Comes by actually doing,
Not just by taking good advice & copying those who already
Experienced "

– Sahaj Sabharwal

Being silent doesn't mean that a person is decent,
It means that the person is a hidden warrior of the
innocents.

– Sahaj Sabharwal

Being silent doesn't mean that a person is decent,
It means that the person is a hidden warrior of the
innocents.

– Sahaj Sabharwal

Don't let your mankind blind
With eyes only, you make anyone, virtually nude.
In reality, cooks crude, for your food.
Lust is the position holder in your mood.
Behaviour with them is really, so rude, you intrudes.
Human with mind, heart you mainly excludes.

– Sahaj Sabharwal

The best gift from life often is
The way to depart from it means death

– Sahaj Sabharwal

If a precious thing is lost
Can help avoid other precious things to be lost
Then it is a worth loss

– Sahaj Sabharwal

Love can never be a part of lust,
It's a matter of heart's trust.

– Sahaj Sabharwal

Harder the warm up,
Easier it will be to resist your potential's
Torn up.

– Sahaj Sabharwal

Learn to walk alone,
Don't make helpers as your backbone

– Sahaj Sabharwal

Hard work goes with pain
And comes with gain.

– Sahaj Sabharwal

A creator has to
ignore criticism
work on feedbacks
be patient for getting results
 display organic creativity

– Sahaj Sabharwal

Three qualities that make you a good writer

1.) Not copying someone's write up.
2.) Writing the truth.
3.) Fearless while writing, being incomparable and unique.

– Sahaj Sabharwal

Be the sky and provide the wings,
To help those who can't dare to fly.

– Sahaj Sabharwal

Choose a new vip path
Neither good nor bad
Its good for good
And bad for bad
Being an assistant of god
Distributing the result of deeds
To all

– Sahaj Sabharwal

Just high thinking and doing nothing must not be a greed
Doing more than your thinking is a need

– Sahaj Sabharwal

Some people are like the sun
Help us with warmth in cold
Make us hot tempered sometimes
Still important for systematic working

– Sahaj Sabharwal

If deep thoughts don't strike,
Your mind, you can't say that you don't like

– Sahaj Sabharwal

Let them leave
Let them leave,
Let's see how trustworthy are those for whom they leave you, for their believe.

– Sahaj Sabharwal

Let yourself
Discovered
The main reason
For which you are still alive

– Sahaj Sabharwal

Miracle is a motivation booster

Which sparkles when you are seen pationate about your work with patience to get results

– Sahaj Sabharwal

For researchers, become a sample

For competitors, become an example

For achievements, respect hard work as a god in a temple

– Sahaj Sabharwal

When we are not getting expected results

We mostly think that we can't do it.

At this point, mostly everyone consider it as waste of time

And stop their efforts into it

After going very near to our goals

We can't fail, just we need is patience

But those who still do it

Even after disappointment,

Keeping hope

And believing in their aim

Gets desired results for sure

As at that place they are so near to their goal

But loss of patience, results to failure

– Sahaj Sabharwal

Fake people
Are just like dead followers on instagram
That just looks good in number
But values nothing

– Sahaj Sabharwal

Believe in you
No person can
Understand or determine you as
A hero or a zero
Because only you can
Experience the condition or the circumstances in which you are in and still living life in your best way

– Sahaj Sabharwal

All of us are stars
All of us are luminous
All of us are creativity of god
But we think that we don't shine as bright
Our brightness is noticed by all around us
Some of the observers
Are like mirror
Shows us our reality and capabilities
And encourages and motivates us
While others are jealous , watches us , enjoys our light
And just ignores to feedback/appreciate

– Sahaj Sabharwal

The best way to forget something
Is to think about it that much that you get bored,
And your mind and heart's core can't bear it anymore.

– Sahaj Sabharwal

My short-term goal in life is
To experience it that much
That i could teach someone about it
And that student of mine could also teach further
well

– Sahaj Sabharwal

To forget your pain
The best way to deal is to heal
By showing the benefits
And the achievements
That couldn't be achieved
Without that pain

– Sahaj Sabharwal

In silence
My mind makes sense

– Sahaj Sabharwal

Bring a change
Which independently you arrange
Everyone thinks of it but ignores as strange
Which everyone want to be a part for exchange
But will get those, whom you approve, reach that range

– Sahaj Sabharwal

The comfortable the dress,
The lower will be the stress.

– Sahaj Sabharwal

When you have
No other option than to wait
Then, don't be late
Even to wait

– Sahaj Sabharwal

Copy the comfort, not style

– Sahaj Sabharwal

If your life is without a wife
It doesn't mean that you rape other women or forcefully ruin someone to become your wife

– Sahaj Sabharwal

Being limitless has no value
Without a boundary

– Sahaj Sabharwal

It's better to be prepared
To get those things which you rarely cared

– Sahaj Sabharwal

Be that much transparent
That if someone tries to use false tricks
Could be caught and surrendered easily

– Sahaj Sabharwal

Rest in hell !
Those who can't care, even the well

– Sahaj Sabharwal

If you take inspiration from someone's success ,
You will get your turn .
If you try to let someone down ,
Out of jealousy , your inbuilt talent will burn .

– Sahaj Sabharwal

Don't wait for good times,
Try to perform your best in bad times.
Take advantage of your problems.
As we require chance and opportunity
To showcase our ability
And that appears at every time as a challenge.
The more the problems, more will be the chances to
showcase and recognise yourself.

— Sahaj Sabharwal

Never try to be stable
Or stuck at a better space
Try to move constantly making yourself that much
capable
That you get the best place

— Sahaj Sabharwal

Declining is not an end,
It's an alert that failure has sent

— Sahaj Sabharwal

Try to become really active
Than to work on the ways to look attractive
To get someone's attention that you are really reactive

— Sahaj Sabharwal

Follow and respect yourself
More than your talent
Because you are the real owner
Of your talent
In fact people will respect and follow you
Only because of your talent

– Sahaj Sabharwal

No need
Of those who misuse you
For their greed

– Sahaj Sabharwal

Try to be steadfast & straightforward that if any
unwanted distractions tries to come on your path,
Get ignored, offended & failed to win you

– Sahaj Sabharwal

Listen to yourself
It's better that you listen to yourself,
Than to allow others to force or confuse you.

- sahaj sabharwal

Just getting a 😝 mask is not a task,
Wearing it properly ✅ is a task, that no one asks. ♂

– Sahaj Sabharwal

Just copy the way to do hard work
Don't copy the whole work

– Sahaj Sabharwal

In actual, no one can compel someone to do
something.
If a person wishes to do it,
He will do it by any means.
If not, he will never do,
You can go to any extent.

– Sahaj Sabharwal

Never humiliate someone
Because everyone is a
Creativity of god and
Making fun of someone is
Making fun of god's creation.

– Sahaj Sabharwal

Just like fire
Help others with
Your heat and bright light
Burn those who bites or fights

– Sahaj Sabharwal

A human with heart
Can feel & understand another person's heart
Need is to get it by heart

– Sahaj Sabharwal

Even hell is well
Than to enjoy someone's
Part of heaven

– Sahaj Sabharwal

Live your life fully,
It's more than to
Live it successfully.
According to your taste,
No need to tell or show
Someone the way you are living,
As it's just time waste.

– Sahaj Sabharwal

I carry my past
As an inspiration
To provide diligent motivational

– Sahaj Sabharwal

Watch at your goal with your unique view & current
position
Not with someone's point of view or position

– Sahaj Sabharwal

I am not stubborn
I am steadfast
And i am proud of it

– Sahaj Sabharwal

The good in you
Can be enlightened
During bad times only

– Sahaj Sabharwal

Never be disappointed that doing everything but you
are nothing today
You will definitely be appointed as the man of
tomorrow due to an all-out effort

– Sahaj Sabharwal

Never trust anyone
Unless you observe it at that particular place
But become a person on whom anyone can believe
and they neither regret their decision nor leave

– Sahaj Sabharwal

You must not look at those
Whom you know are in a problem
But you can neither help them nor solve their
problem
But you are just acting as salt on wounds
And they just feel embarrassed and despondent when
you do so

– Sahaj Sabharwal

No matter, how you deal it,
But it's worthless, if you can't take time to feel it.

– Sahaj Sabharwal

When I was a child,
I never imagined that life is so wild.

– Sahaj Sabharwal

Everyone can write
But for wrong & right
Only a great writer can fight

– Sahaj Sabharwal

Try to win heart, not mind
Because mind is blind
But heart is always kind

– Sahaj Sabharwal

No need of long indirect
Texts when just one word
Is enough to describe it

– Sahaj Sabharwal

Inner voice is a voice
Which expels when no choice.
Tolerance is silent inside noise
Which becomes dangerous crime's base.

– Sahaj Sabharwal

Failure is the best result to get rid of forfeiture ego

– Sahaj Sabharwal

Utilize your life
Keep changing yourself
Learn to be brave to take risks
Not with the fear that you may lose the present good you
But with the hope that you might discover a better you

– Sahaj Sabharwal

It's quite unfair but unfeigned
That less get less
And already more get more
But if deserving less get more
And undeserving more get less
This can avoid worthless stress and everyone will feel
laudably blessed

– Sahaj Sabharwal

No one will notice the common things
But no one will forget the distinctive things
Be glad to be mad about those things which everyone
considers as strange and out of shyness loses to be
unique

– Sahaj Sabharwal

When I am in doubt
I try to solve it and not
Just making an illogical pout

– Sahaj Sabharwal

It's better to take time
To be in mood than to waste time doing the same
thing with a rude or apathetic attitude

– Sahaj Sabharwal

A creative person doesn't require
Any already established platform
That creativity alone is enough to bang to make any
platform an established one

— Sahaj Sabharwal

It's better to initiate first
Than to regret being late due to some blunder at the
time of ultimate presentation

— Sahaj Sabharwal

Never underestimate even a lucid originator because
he may be worthless for the viewer
But the person in that particular field can only
understand the complex thinking or toil behind it

— Sahaj Sabharwal

Those who speak loud
It doesn't mean that they are impolite or headstrong
It means that they have their presence on their point,
are loyal to themselves and are fearless as they are true
Not like those who speak so soft that their talks could
be ignored as faint

— Sahaj Sabharwal

Never force yourself
To hide yourself

– Sahaj Sabharwal

Never spare those
Who don't care
God's beautiful creation
Means you (human)

– Sahaj Sabharwal

Real nature lover is that who love even the natural
disasters which seems to be fatal

– Sahaj Sabharwal

Watch at every human with
His/her primary humanity characteristics
Not after discriminating/judging his/her secondary
characteristics

– Sahaj Sabharwal

Never break their trust
Who were with you when
Everyone was ashamed to stand with you
And never trust those who left you earlier
But want to be with you when
You found your own value
And they were just attracted out of egocentricity

– Sahaj Sabharwal

Never deny even a false blame as
You can use it as a challenge
For you to improve yourself
And put in more efforts as
A mock test to prove

– Sahaj Sabharwal

Nowadays
I judge people by
The way they wears
And manages face masks

– Sahaj Sabharwal

When the complex future becomes a difficult
question
Only the powerful past's signature acts as an
acknowledgement as a one word substitution solution

– Sahaj Sabharwal

Handle with care
Every heart requires some time to become a
trustworthy part and ignoring after adding to your
cart may result in a dejected depart

– Sahaj Sabharwal

The place i am looking for
Is far away from here
But you all will be there

– Sahaj Sabharwal

Winning something by cheating
Will make your mind feel glad in the interim,
Will make beguiled people accolade you for winning
their superstitious hearts,
But will make you lose the most important thing -
winning your conscious heart!
On account of dissatisfaction and self-disloyalty

- Sahaj Sabharwal

Welcome advice from all & do what you yourself
check & pass to be undertaken considering the
opinion of others

- Sahaj Sabharwal

Your eyes can see everything but ignores
Your mind trusts on your eyes and explores
Your core trusts no one but feels and deals
judgmatically to implore

- Sahaj Sabharwal

We live in a world where
People consider just watching and dissolving some
crime
As problem solving
And those who are fighting for truth
And revealing the truth are considered
As boring noobs so mad

- Sahaj Sabharwal

No one can stop himself from putting enough efforts, if he
Already knows that the results
Will be guaranteed satisfactory.
All we need is to keep hope to
Put enough efforts to get
Auspicious results

– Sahaj Sabharwal

Why to have a fear after you watch an energetic performance
And feels hare-brained due to bleakness
Just be selfish to extract your motivational point from it and
Perform in such a way that your dynamic performance becomes a result changer and establishes the next level

– Sahaj Sabharwal

Never be dependent on someone
Because when you depend on someone you are making someone the emperor of your kingdom
And everyone will be selfish and will look for his/her benefits at the first priority that's why it's better to be a jack of all trades and hence the king of your own land

– Sahaj Sabharwal

Death is just a physical end
But we'll pray to god to unite us again afterlife

– Sahaj Sabharwal

To write your future
You have to earn enough ink and
Should learn to maintain your
Pen under any circumstances

– Sahaj Sabharwal

Never compromise with your integrity by virtue of embarrassment because when you are protecting your personal right, you must give priority to yourself rather than to take decision on the pressure of mortifying public, that will be temporary. But the effect of your decision will be permanent.

– Sahaj Sabharwal

Be strong enough to cope up with wrong people so that they can't force you to convert you into their category over time.

– Sahaj Sabharwal

Your haters are your biggest fans◌

* They will be the first to watch and dislike your latest creativity

* They will analyze your performance carefully, which shows their consciousness as impression

* They will compare themselves with you and will try to prove themselves more than you as you are a role model for them

* They will work on you for free by sharing your content to some more haters so that they make fun of it and dislike too, which will increase the number of shares and reach for making it viral

– Sahaj Sabharwal

Fly with your talent/ability
Not with the dependency on promotion/propaganda
– Sahaj Sabharwal

Ups & downs are the only proof
That you are moving constantly on your path
And your actions are showing lively reactions
– Sahaj Sabharwal

Try not to lose hope even after an insult

As it may be a chance to make a joke for the foolish people but for you it is the best opportunity to improve your result

- Sahaj Sabharwal

When you are doing your work with full devotion

And still some jealous people continuously plays with your kind emotion then you must become a helper to fight for peace to provide them the result of their deeds irrespective of commotion because emotional peace must be your first priority

- Sahaj Sabharwal

Be proud that you found someone at a greater level than that of your's

Because it will make you feel jealous

And jealousy is the key to do something more as a motivation

- Sahaj Sabharwal

In appetence of things you don't have,

Please don't ignore to convert the things you already have into deprived ones

- Sahaj Sabharwal

Practicing struggle before success is the same as taking salad before a meal that can be taken along with or after the meal but taking it before a meal have extra benefits if you have to eat it

– Sahaj Sabharwal

Only you know your real status
But you can show others the way you want them to see it that may be fake to get fake acclaim with respect to yourself or it may be real you to show what you really are being unbiased.
So, there is no need to show fake things to impress others unless it can't impress even you

– Sahaj Sabharwal

Be positive
People think that to succeed is the most difficult thing and just demand their growth but they don't know that whenever there is a good thing, a negative thing will always be it's part
And to maintain yourself after you succeed is a really difficult thing because criticism and other negativity is always there. You just have to try to be more positive to be capable to bear/ignore the criticism that is just like a mock test that you have to pass by continuing to be positive.

– Sahaj Sabharwal

Thinking to do something more than your efficiency, will make you distressed

Thinking to do something less than your efficiency, will make you negligent and unsatisfied

Thinking to do something at your known level, will definitely help you do more than your capability as a bonus and that too in the best manner

– Sahaj Sabharwal

Talent is not an extraordinary quality.

It is just a simple quality present in every living being but the one who is able to express his/her quality uninhibitedly is termed as a talented being.

– Sahaj Sabharwal

To learn good things, you must have full knowledge about bad things first because having full knowledge of bad things already justifies/answers why you shouldn't apply/follow them

– Sahaj Sabharwal

Currently, the circumstances are such that people will make you late by wasting your time not with the purpose that they want to know your condition but they just want to create confusions and tensions in your straight path and later on you will get to know that your own decision was much better than those who were trying to confuse you.

Thus, you must take decision that is much trustworthy and rightful so that you will remain on your particular decision and no external power can ever distract you from your path.

– Sahaj Sabharwal

Those who ask you to prove, they just want to see how you did it but will never accept it. They will just burn your confidence if you will make them jealous.

So, it's better to be transparent with the right people to maintain your self confidence.

– Sahaj Sabharwal

The authentic love never crashes on a trial and denial as a result

It is an assertiveness that provides you an exquisite gift as a new lease of life

– Sahaj Sabharwal

Imperfection is the major characteristic of a human being

But we can still try our best for the finest correction

– Sahaj Sabharwal

Every creation of god has its own value

if you ask a writer, he will say that an artist has more value or vice versa.

if you ask a singer, he will say that a videographer/photographer has more value or vice versa.

if you ask a scientist, he will say that a manufacturer has more value or vice versa.

if you ask a chef, he will say that a grocer has more value or vice versa.

but if you ask common people/audience/receivers, they will say that for them everyone of these has their own value and absence of any one of these will make their lives incomplete and boring

– Sahaj Sabharwal

Mindset matters

On your birthday, you may feel so happy thinking that you are now grown up and have gained good experience up to your age.

At the same time, you may feel so sad thinking that one more year is deducted out of your total years of life and you are getting closer to death and all your gained experience as well as achievements will be physically lost.

It's totally up to you, how you take it.

– Sahaj Sabharwal

Everything has a 50% probability before we get a glimpse of the result as nope or scope

– Sahaj Sabharwal

If you didn't get unsatisfied results where you deserve, then you couldn't be at this position to explore more good and unique ideas as your part of struggle and you couldn't get this much time and things to learn than that of choosing one simple/common step to success.

– Sahaj Sabharwal

It all depends upon our stars

We can even get unexpected things or we can't get even expected things.

– Sahaj Sabharwal

When you yourself are living in a good condition, then your comments on those living in a bad condition can never be valuable and vice versa.

If you want that your comments should be relevant, then you must have to bear their blood in your body to have a feel of their situation and vice versa.

– Sahaj Sabharwal

The beauty of success with which you get impressed easily,

You can't imagine the ugly blood, sweat and tears behind it with which the physical look of success looks splendid.

Similarly, the creator's background may or may not be that much beautiful, but the creativity is patently adorable.

– Sahaj Sabharwal

The power of karma as hell

Those who are winning their exam of life by cheating just like in an exam from home (online), they will get to know their real failure at the time of their real physical application.

– Sahaj Sabharwal

PROMOTION

Even promotion suits those who have something special in them to show.

Doing promotion is not a bad thing if you have those qualities, for which you need feedback but not getting expected/deserving response. As feedback/response is very important to keep yourself self motivated that you are putting some efforts and those efforts by you are alive in front of your audience too. It will help you to grow yourself by inducing some confidence in you.

– Sahaj Sabharwal

Why should you feel awkward when -:

You sweat

Your body produces smell after sweat

You emit flatulent gases

Or any other natural process occurs

It's a normal thing.

If you are a real being, you will have these characteristics, normally.

You should be cheerful that your body is working well enough to have all these natural abilities.

Hiding your natural processes using man made creations is just hiding your real human activities.

– Sahaj Sabharwal

This new year-2021

➢ Try to take the residue of the year 2020 as a great organic usage for the year 2021.

➢ Try to end your ego, wrong attitude, inhuman activities and over confidence as you can't imagine which year will turn out to be hell for you as an attack of karma(deeds).

➢ Try not to forget the things learnt in the year 2020 especially not to discriminate in anything as when there was a wide gap between rich and poor commonly in any field by miracle of the almighty have survived at a common border.

– Sahaj Sabharwal

It's your mistake
Being good with unworthy bad people is not their mistake as it's savor for them,
It's your mistake as you aren't getting expected reaction.

– Sahaj Sabharwal

Being a human,
"Those who were feeling blithesome when you were futile as a lame,
They can never be heartedly happy with your name and fame when you notch up your game."

– Sahaj Sabharwal

Nowadays, everyone is interested to know about other's aim and the things for which they will apply in future,
But still none of them know exactly about their own future.

A common person will appreciate you if you pass and will ask you about your lifestyle, you opted and will criticize you if you fail in something and have nothing to do with the reason or problem.

But an erudite person will appreciate your efforts in the thing in which you failed and will ask the reason and provide you the good solution and he will give the least priority to the thing you achieved out of what you applied.

As applying as a try is the most important thing, irrespective of you win or lose.

– Sahaj Sabharwal

Definition of my name, With respect to me
Simple and small in look, not in thinking and works
Achiever, achieving myself
(my heart)
Hard hearted with heartless people
Authentic personality with antique value
Jammy because I live in Jammu city, J&K, India

– Sahaj Sabharwal

Fake smile can't care
Sharing a fake smile to make someone feel good and relaxed that you care them is worthless, if you are trying it with a person with a heart, he can't really feel it.
Because those who really cares,
Always show a real smile or no smile.
But still the cared person can feel the hospitality from the heart.

– Sahaj Sabharwal

Self-centred people are those who will enjoy you only if you will talk about them but will get bored easily or will pay no attention when you talk about yourself in front of them

– Sahaj Sabharwal

" Love is a beauty
But beauty is not love "

– Sahaj Sabharwal

Trust yourself - just confidence matters

Please don't hide yourself in fear of those whom you don't even know that they are greater than, equal to or less than you. They might be eagerly waiting for that very thing that you have, but hidden out of hesitation.

– Sahaj Sabharwal

Nowadays, circumstances are trying to prove that superficially attractive appearance is prepotent as compared to the content you present

– Sahaj Sabharwal

CHOICE

Make your choice as your unfiltered voice after which you rejoice because it's totally bootless to make someone happy with your fake choice if you yourself are not happy.

– Sahaj Sabharwal

There are many common intentions which we all want to and must undergo to achieve something. But those who prefer to satisfy their ego first, are left behind even though they have good acumen, being conceit.

– Sahaj Sabharwal

Every under development phase is interesting except that one which is bored as well developed.

– Sahaj Sabharwal

She: why are you so late to respond to my messages? Ignoring?

He: i don't want to miss a single precious message from your side so if i see your message, i mark it as unread so that i don't just check it hastily or dismiss like i do for others

She: sad

– Sahaj Sabharwal

No one will notice you when you are doing even a brawny work, normally but everyone will heed you when you are trying to hide even a minor thing via peculiar behaviour

– Sahaj Sabharwal

The world is waiting for you to be a change maker. No one else will come here to set an example before you.
And everyone will come to believe you after you did it.

– Sahaj Sabharwal

The world i am lost in
Is a new and profound one.
You will also come here soon with time.
Just for making it easy for you, i am here, collecting and sending some data for your future help, so that you don't get lost like me.

– Sahaj Sabharwal

Messy people just know how to tamper with our business, switching us on, to prove ourselves, in which we improve a lot. But they don't know how to stop us, when we put our efforts and get proved. Hence, we achieve heights being unbeatable, as a plus point for us.

– Sahaj Sabharwal

Do things with pleasure
Not with formality
Even if the thing is a formality
Decide to do everything with joy
Rather than to be annoyed. Enjoy!

– Sahaj Sabharwal

Success is when your inimitable thoughts become facts
And those stunning facts have a life changing influence over someone's life.

– Sahaj Sabharwal

Oh, God!

Don't pray to God to get only good things.
Pray to god to help you pick out good/right things out of bad/wrong things.

For example-: in multiple choice questions, if you just learn/observe the correct option, ignoring the wrong choices, you will get confused when similar looking wrong options will appear in exam.

So, you must know which option is wrong and why and which option is correct and why to excel an exam.

– Sahaj Sabharwal

Expressing isn't show-off

Hiding yourself from the world

Thinking that expressing yourself is a kind of show-off is a totally wrong mentality. If you will not show your presence or stay hidden in your entire life, this world will remove your identity and will hide you. And all your inner talents will never be appreciated. When you will be aware of it, getting nothing being hidden, your lifetime might have been over to regret. So, express yourself freely, you have taken birth to do and show something, not to hide something.

– Sahaj Sabharwal

Don't allow anyone to help you to stand up once again when you fell down if you really want to learn something on your own

– Sahaj Sabharwal

Lowliness is not a problem

But neglecting from the present position really hurts

– Sahaj Sabharwal

It's normal that new people will join you and old people will support you if you win

But those who support and motivate you even if you lose to make you win are your real admirers

– Sahaj Sabharwal

Small items/services are those on whom big items/services are totally dependent, which everyone wants in their everyday life but no one wants to pay for them. Because people are never satisfied to provide them a value.

– Sahaj Sabharwal

Every unknown personality is not anonymous

– Sahaj Sabharwal

You are giving your best in everything

You are getting nothing from everything.

Don't worry, god is trying to arrange the greatest of all time shot for you.

An incredible miracle will provide you the befitting enjoyment of life.

It will change your whole life.

Be calm and keep it up.

Time will come soon.

I have seen it.

I believe in it.

You will soon believe in it.

– Sahaj Sabharwal

Efforts aggravate during the earlier journey only. After that period, you will be relaxed to forget them but their result will always be with you like blessings.

– Sahaj Sabharwal

UNIFORM IS VARYING

We all know that wearing a uniform means wearing a dress which makes everyone look equal as it's name indicates. But nowadays, uniforms are also divided into different categories based on qualities, quantities, ways of wearing and usage of avoidable boastful things along with uniform. Many of us might have noticed that those who buy/wear new uniforms every moment, tries to look superior to those wearing older one, even in uniforms. These divisions are the reasons behind inequality, dishonouring uniform.

– Sahaj Sabharwal

Taking and solving unnecessary tension makes your mind sharp rather than stress/depression if you could bear to do so.

– Sahaj Sabharwal

People would love to read those writings which they understand easily whether they are copied or changed with some synonyms or are on a similar trending theme. But when the content is quite unique means organic, then people either don't agree with it or consider it as not good because they aren't interested to give time to learn something new.

– Sahaj Sabharwal

TRUTH

If you don't deserve something,
You will never get it.
And if you get it by any means,
It will be snatched from you
By fair means or foul.

– Sahaj Sabharwal

Happiness is like a feather
Will fly high until you flow freely
With all the circumstances you face
But when it fell down as a sad event
You have to push yourself up on your own
As an initiative to live happy life again.

– Sahaj Sabharwal

IGNORE THEM

These people will never support you when you are in your growing stage. You will grow on your own strength. But they will smarm you and will never leave you when you are grown-up as famous personality. Ignore these

– Sahaj Sabharwal

Taking enough time for fulfilling heart's trust and mind's lust is worthwhile as it's impact will be on lifetime

– Sahaj Sabharwal

WORK TIME

To do something flawlessly
The best way is to forget your kinship related to your work for a while and work seriously on the basis of equality with an alien

– Sahaj Sabharwal

DON'T WASTE YOUR LIFE

You can save yourself
Try to learn to swim
Don't say that your
Life will be over soon
Life is unique don't waste it

– Sahaj Sabharwal

Everyone will ignore
Until you become the one
After following whom others will care

– Sahaj Sabharwal

The thing you rejected in one time,
Was selected by my heart after being rejected many times.
Please don't be so quick to dismiss the efforts. Efforts deserves realization

– Sahaj Sabharwal

😄 BUSY PEOPLE 😄

These are busy sarcastic people
They do nothing but lollygagging
They explore and discover
Other busy people just like them
And this busy schedule goes on

– Sahaj Sabharwal

If you are really willing to ignore him
Then please don't look at him a single time
It really hurts, when you look first and then ignore, to
evade being sighted.

– Sahaj Sabharwal

Accreditation is not an imperceptible thing that you
ask and demean if somebody needs it or not.
It's an authenticity that every exemplary creature
deserves and he must be given.
That's lucid.

– Sahaj Sabharwal

OVER CONFIDENCE ↓↓100

Most of us consider Over Confidence (Over Positivity) as a negative term.

But in reality, it is an excellent thing that anyone can achieve easily, if you can thrive to manage it which can be difficult but not impossible.

As Over Confidence may have to failure

But neither for every time nor for everyone.

And negativity is a part of our life so we can try to dominate positivity so that the effect of negativity can be neglected.

– Sahaj Sabharwal

It's my thought and a fact that

Whenever you have superfluity of something, you will be satisfied enough to utilize its less quantity

And when you have something in less quantity that is approximately equal to the quality you actually require, you will use its full quantity and still you will be unsatisfied due to greed

– Sahaj Sabharwal

ENJOY NOW 

Enjoy and celebrate even little achievements in your life Because when you will achieve more in future and will be at a higher level, you will consider your past achievements as that must small that you will ignore them and will laugh at what you were celebrating and enjoying before as your greatest.

– Sahaj Sabharwal

MOOD

When you are in a good mood,
You will find interest even in a dummy thing.
But when you are not in the mood,
You will not like even your favourite thing.

– Sahaj Sabharwal

FILMY VIEW OF LIFE

God is a compulsory FINAL EXAM

Everyone must attempt

Priest, Guru or Prophet are the TEACHERS

These teachers claims to make you pass this exam of life easily by taking tuitions from them.

But after experiencing their tuitions only, a student can provide feedback to upcoming students.

Some of these teachers or their students are really good or sometimes bad and vice versa

But taking tuitions is not compulsory

One can pass this exam without the help of a teacher on his/her own too.

– Sahaj Sabharwal

Postulation says

Almighty God & Demon coexist

When and where the surroundings are in its most ideal situation

– Sahaj Sabharwal

REALISE✦

I am not saying that
Do wrong things and don't tell me
I am saying that
Do good things and don't even tell me

– Sahaj Sabharwal

Changing world with the trend,
Can never be a genuine reason.
But with the change in trend,
If you can't challenge your mindset,
If you can't update your vision,
Blame yourself because you are
Mature enough to understand
The Change in the clothing
With the change in seasons.
It's a similar case.

– Sahaj Sabharwal

If you get an innovative idea

Then try to work on it as soon as possible

Because after some time after deep thinking, when you will think to do it,

An inside worm full of demotivation/negativity will take birth inside you which try its best to stop you from doing it.

So, don't think much

Do it now.

– Sahaj Sabharwal

UTILISE YOUR NEGATIVITY

Negativity can never end as a zero value

It will be present even inside favorableness

But you can use it to be positive by ignoring it

You are so quick & smart in ignoring

So, ignore hell not heaven

– Sahaj Sabharwal

IT'S AN IMMORTAL TRUTH
RELATIONSHIP IS JUST A PAIR
MATCHING A HUMANE PAIR IS RARE
NOWADAYS, EXCEPT ALTRUISTIC
TEACHERS AND PARENTS SOMEONE
RARELY CARES

– Sahaj Sabharwal

Some special messages
Don't need to be in a formal format preference is given to that deep special messages for which they are given this special allowance

– Sahaj Sabharwal

YOUR INTELLECT ⬛ IS STILL STUCKED IN CHILDHOOD☺

If you consider yourself as right,

Even if you know that you are wrong.

If you consider others as wrong,

Even if you know that they are right.

– Sahaj Sabharwal

Bad People are not really Bad

They are a good source of motivation

The good in them is even superior than those of the good people but hidden because of the bad things they do.

– Sahaj Sabharwal

They uphold it only as Formality

Because in this new world, the term " Heartily Attachment " is totally extinct

– Sahaj Sabharwal

Most of us are blind to respect only those who are recognized ones

We appreciate those who are recognized or those who know how to apply for something

Not those who are unrecognized or don't know how to apply and due to some issues those who can't apply to be recognized but are really more talented/ deserving than the recognized ones

For already discovered ones, we explore

For Undiscovered talented we simply ignore

– Sahaj Sabharwal

" Never compromise with true love
To be loved "

– Sahaj Sabharwal

Life is like a two wheeler
You will balance only when you start riding You can choose any speed to reach your destination depending on your comfort and safety
You should never stop or waver when you see other vehicles around you overtaking you or moving faster than you Because this may detract your present speed too This will not affect their speed So, it's better to keep moving

– Sahaj Sabharwal

You also have the same intention
But when you hear it from someone's mouth
You make him feel awkward

– Sahaj Sabharwal

Being kind with hardness
Why to trust a stranger just with fake outer characteristics?
You are providing them a chance as an opportunity to break your trust forever

– Sahaj Sabharwal

To wait for someone
And to be late for no reason
Can never show real favour or empathy
But it shows foolishness
Because a real caring person
Will never compel you to wait for him
Or to be late with him
He will always advice you to carry on
As you need not to suffer or loose
With someone's mistake

– Sahaj Sabharwal

A person is penurious
With a striking goal
To be a gracious future spendthrift

– Sahaj Sabharwal

It's Me
My Style is my trend is my proud is my uniqueness
- Sahaj Sabharwal

When you try to be over smart
And tell something opposite or exaggerate from the
orignal extremity
Due to which you get into trouble
Most of the times you will get unexpected results
And unfortunately, the tide turns and you will not get
the deserving response
That's why, tell only what actually it is
To really get rid of extra scuffle
- Sahaj Sabharwal

Not a bad attitude I swear 🌐💯
On the same hand, not bearing a bad attitude, have
that fear if it's not clear 😊🔥
- Sahaj Sabharwal

Maturity is when
You begin to face and are forced by
Yourself to follow those things which
You were unable to understand when
Your experienced elders were giving
You a glimpse of those.
- Sahaj Sabharwal

No one feels good in a bad situation
But the circumstances make you strong
To adopt it and convert survival to living

- Sahaj Sabharwal

You are that person who can find negativity even in
an extremely positive situation
Then why you fail easily to find positivity even in a
neutral situation?
You can find positivity too
But your mindset is not flexible to find it
Work on it to make it virtuous

- Sahaj Sabharwal

Already poor people have to suffer with tremendous shortage of money

Already weak people in something have to suffer with unstoppable falling off results

Already demotivated people have to suffer with further disappointment

Already late people have to suffer with long-standing shortage of time

Mostly, it happens as it is and it should be

But all you need is to be exceptional

As it is not easy to be a game changer

To get exceptional results even if you are not that perfect by inducing special skills

To have your favourite results as your dream come true

It is quite rare to do so

But not impossible

You have to be rare

If you really care not only yourself

But your die hard dreams

– Sahaj Sabharwal

Every Confidence is an Overconfidence

Before it pass through the final strict negative part of your thoughts, making it better to succeed.

– Sahaj Sabharwal

SHOW WHAT YOU REALLY ARE

If you try to show a fake pretension
You are the most innocent person
As you are showing your good side only
And that too fake one
You are not even loyal to yourself
As if you show your good side
People will only appreciate you for some time with which you will become careless and overconfident
With which you can't improve to make your good side the best
And if you show your bad side too,
People will help you to eliminate that bad side through criticism
And then you can become the best

– Sahaj Sabharwal

Fake love-: When you go far away physically and forget that lovely person
True love-: When you go far away physically and come more nearer heartedly to your love

– Sahaj Sabharwal

If you are good at your place
Try to make others good too
Because if you contribute your best at your place
And they will do bad to you
As they don't have positive mindset like you
It will have an irreversible affect on you, indirectly
So, Doing good may or may not have good in return
You have to make it good as a result improving
volunteer

– Sahaj Sabharwal

They ping you
Because you have a great value
They sting you
Because their jealousy bites them
As you have made your value more than they have.

– Sahaj Sabharwal

NEVER BE FULLY SATISFIED

Dissatisfaction is the only reason
That you are still moving
If you were satisfied after fulfilling just initial/smaller
goals without making and trying to fulfill
new/challenging goals
You would have stopped/left a long time ago

– Sahaj Sabharwal

At a particular moment,
When there is no one for you to care
Then, your inner soul gives rise to self-consciousness
– Sahaj Sabharwal

Never copy good people
Just to check whether people like you too
Become an updated version of yourself
To know how many real people really like the real you
– Sahaj Sabharwal

Out of sluggishness,
Please don't defame life
That its nothing but boring
Speak the unconcealable truth
That it is that much interestingly vast
That you are unable to explore all
So you feel better leave it and blame life
As there are many energetic explorers
Who will check your reviews
And feel demotivated for nothing
– Sahaj Sabharwal

Isn't it ?

Reality Says

Those things which you do in your daily routine

You rarely thought or knew or noticed what and how you are doing that particular thing

Because you have done that much practice that you can do that work even after closing your eyes or without thinking much about it

– Sahaj Sabharwal

Don't be selfish ☠✖↓↓

Even with yourself

Never leave your heart alone

During bad times

Otherwise your heart will leave you

During your good times

And good times are impossible

Without a heart

– Sahaj Sabharwal

When you have ultimate powers

They're dangerous for your problems

But when you can't control them

They'll become dangerous for you only

– Sahaj Sabharwal

If you ask
For my choices, you have to do that particular task
Otherwise, no fake formalities
No need to ask
Do whatever you want

– Sahaj Sabharwal

Probability of failure
Is even in high probability of success
But if you prefer to think
Only about failure by ignoring success
Then out of fear of failure
You will be unable to do even a single Simple work in which
You could succeed easily

– Sahaj Sabharwal

Everyone has an equal value still
Frivolous thinking people
Will feel humiliated
Even in standing with the lower class people with whom they are higher today.
Perfect mindset people
Will provide value to the lower class
Help them grow/stand heigher.
Notice the thinking,
Mindset matters.

– Sahaj Sabharwal

You are doing something beyond their thinking.
They will ask for results but not hard work as a proof.
No problem, they will also be satisfied with time.
Soon, you will turn your practice into success.
You are doing it, you need to know better, not them.
You are satisfied with what you are doing.
That's more than enough.
Keep up the good work.

– Sahaj Sabharwal

When you do something independently
Its your unique creation
Obviously you will love it
Because its your own
And you know the level of hard work
You did to achieve it
So, you will never dislike it at any extent
But the feedback by your heart for you
May or may not be true for others
People's negative feedback
Provides us an idea of the mistakes we did
Because only outside party can notice our silly mistakes
Their eyes will be only in searching mistakes by
ignoring the good in you
And good people will let you know the valuable feedback
Because reality is always valuable

– Sahaj Sabharwal

Hurt your ego
Otherwise your ego will hurt you soon.
Why shouldn't you
Respect for Respect
Like for Like
Feedback for Feedback
Support for Support
Even in the earlier stages
When you have/are nothing
You don't deserve to get/be anything
But your ego is forcing you
To show that you are something
Or you have something
So you are unable to get even those things which you
could get, being calm
Otherwise who are you?
Why should people do the same for you?
Why should they provide you respect or fame?
Why shouldn't you get an unfollow when you
unfollow or not follow someone?
These show off tips work
When you really did something great
And you found your real value
At that time, even ego will become
Your responsibility
And everyone will be really proud of you
You will get everything even without fake barter formalities

– Sahaj Sabharwal

A brand without a value
Is just like a truth without a reality

– Sahaj Sabharwal

FOLLOW YOUR PASSION BECAUSE
PASSION IS YOUR VIRTUAL DREAM
THIS VIRTUAL DREAM IS GOING
TO FULFILL YOUR AIM IN LIFE

– Sahaj Sabharwal

Level up your talent that much high that
Your destiny must not suffer with lack of luck
Your destiny will support you that much that
You will not suffer with lack of talent

– Sahaj Sabharwal

Nothing is fake
If you're really real and vice-versa

– Sahaj Sabharwal

Nowadays,
Innocent eyes 👁
Clever mind 🧠
And naughty exploits
Are new characteristics 💪
Of a cute personality 🐭

– Sahaj Sabharwal

Hey, Don't call the aged people
As the blunt people
These people are just like
Water in an ocean of knowledge
And you are just a beginner now
You're not even a single drop of it
So you don't even know that how
Much deep and widespread
Is the water in that ocean
You will learn from their sharp
Reach of knowledge with time
Their ageing faces might not seem
Good to you, but the value behind that Face is a well
experienced personality.

– Sahaj Sabharwal

Good is to come
Only on one condition
You have to be patient
You don't have to go

– Sahaj Sabharwal

FAILURE
Earlier you were not selected being ineligible
SUCCESS
Now you are not selecting the ineligible

– Sahaj Sabharwal

It's sour but the truth that
" Being Selfish is Self Caring "
And if you really care for yourself
It's more than enough to stay happy

– Sahaj Sabharwal

You are shy, that's fine
But don't make your shyness
The reason behind you lose
A great opportunity

– Sahaj Sabharwal

Wait for a Good Vibe 
If you think something is good
But you are not in mood to dig it.
Wait for a moment till you are in a good vibe. It's guaranteed that you will give time to adore it.
Don't be in hurry to feel it.
To avoid pathetic results.

– Sahaj Sabharwal

If you care for someone
As you love that person
More than that of yours
You're really doing a wrong thing
Because if you will be great
Then only you will be able to
Take care of your lovely person
In future too. And that's true hospitality.

– Sahaj Sabharwal

Keep struggling for your demands
But never lose at an extent of compromising

– Sahaj Sabharwal

Your life is really not fine, when you do wrong things and get right results. If you're getting good after doing bad, then there is also a probability of getting bad even after doing good. So, don't be fully satisfied. At least don't cheat yourself. As it may be right with respect to you but it's always problematic with respect to Karma.

– Sahaj Sabharwal

Manual scandals are natural.
They're not in somebody's hand.
The more, the scandals occur,
The more you will learn to explore.
And not by depressing your mind,
But by experiencing your clever mind.
To discover and enjoy the miracle.

– Sahaj Sabharwal

Dear Mate,
Circumstances made you wait.
That wait was not to make you late.
But to help you improve further till the results were delayed.
And to get even higher than the expected for which you prayed.
Intentions were to create pressure to pump you jump higher, not to slump, being stressed :)

– Sahaj Sabharwal

Vexation can affect you up to
A certain limit and that
Limit is in your hand

– Sahaj Sabharwal

Do u Agree 
Keep Working
To Avoid Jerking

– Sahaj Sabharwal

Being abnormal is a bad word in our society.

People just tease an abnormal person.

But when an abnormal person do those wonders that a normal person can't even try,

Trust me, it's just a prodigy sent by the Almighty just to clear your misconception and to declare their worth as compared to normal you.

– Sahaj Sabharwal

You complain that they view,

But are not liking.

You complain that they like,

But are not commenting.

You complain that they like and comment,

But are not sharing.

But what about those who are not even viewing,

So that your post's impression or reach or views don't go high.

They are your egotistical haters.

In actual, they love your content and get inspired that much that they believe that your post will be having a high level as usual.

Your success is making them jealous.

That means you really did a great job.

That's why, those people are your real fans turn motivators.

– Sahaj Sabharwal

You lost your toss

You lost your chance

At last, You were going to lose your game

But the flame of hope was still alive

That was your biggest win

As you were defamed being wilful

You proved this quality of yours in a good manner,

By combating with failure to win your fame back

Only that made you to win the lost game with a miracle

– Sahaj Sabharwal

▓ BEWARE ▓

A thief don't have a different face

He may be any one of us and even you

Anybody who need something that you have, But he can't get it by himself due to some reason, He may try to steal it

Any person can steal, trust no one

Even a thief is fearful of you & vice-versa

– Sahaj Sabharwal

You changed for the lust of physical love
But real love still stands as the truth
It never changes for the physiological you

— Sahaj Sabharwal

CAN YOU RELATE ? 

The most creative thoughts appears
When you are trying to concentrate on something different but important,

As a distraction for your mind or you can say it's a miracle.

But you must know how to manage to extract the quality content from it so as to produce something creative and not ignoring or disrespecting the thing with which you came to think up to this extent.

— Sahaj Sabharwal

Some past experiences might seem bad, But their outcome can make your future feel so glad

— Sahaj Sabharwal

IT'S REALITY 💯 💯 OF REAL LIFE 🔥 🔥

Simple life seems like living dead.

Unexpected shocks are natural but important in life.

These shocks can keep you alive and can perish you too.

You have to bear to survive. It's reality of real life.

– Sahaj Sabharwal

SHOUT-OUT TO SUPER WOMAN 👩🏻 ♀

Doing everything but not even getting acknowledgement or praise and not even asking for it.

She did a lot and is still compromising,

Only because she is a super woman, your mom or your wife.

If it was life at her place,

You would have been renounced a long time ago.

And even you would have flattered life, just to impress to live it.

It's better to make super women as your life.

Provide authority and respect to her too. She is also human like you. Stop crimes against her. Keep her happy and blessed too.

– Sahaj Sabharwal

YOU ARE A STAR ☆ ✨

Some people with grouchy mood,
Will come on the way, in your life,
To make your mood bad.
But you are a star.
Many people need your brightness.
You are important to them.
You must ignore those bad moody people.
To keep your mood good.
And to keep shining as always.

– Sahaj Sabharwal

MY THOUGHTS ✏️ 💊

Just like a painkiller drug,
That do nothing but fools your mind,
Just to make you feel that your pain is over.
But in actual, it is still there.
And you get virtual relief.
Make your heart capable of making
Your mind fool to handle any difficult situation.
Considering that your negativity, to fail or lose is no more.
So that you can concentrate well and bring outstanding results even in a difficult situation.

– Sahaj Sabharwal

Make your attitude like

you have to do it, as it's your passion. And your hard
work have to concentrate on your dream, as it's your
aim in life.

No compromise at all.

– Sahaj Sabharwal

Don't become fake
Just to impress others
If you are really real
Win to impress yourself first

– Sahaj Sabharwal

ज़िंदगी तो मौत का एकमात्र खाना है,

मजबूरी मे, आज नही तो कल सबको निगल जाना है।

इंसान का काम तो मेहनत कर, जीवन सजाना है, तब भी

थमना नही साथियों, किसी का पेट भर, पुण्य काम कर,

कारण तो केवल एक बहाना है।

– सहज सभरवाल

बुरे काम करके, बुद्धि को देते दाम हैं।

अच्छी तरह जानते, आगे रस्ता जाम, सब नाकाम है।

अच्छे काम को करके भी, जैसे करते अहसान हैं।

हितैषी-दिल, खुदा से फिर भी कहता,

ये हैवान नहीं, अनजान हैं।

- सहज सभरवाल

जो डर गए हम

जब आए थे गम

करके आंखें नम

आनंद लेते आज भी पुरानी

गलतियों में था दम

आज उनसे सीख गए हम

मेरे सनम

- सहज सभरवाल

यूँ मांगिये मत,

देने की चाह रखिए।

यूँ दीजिये मत,

दान सहित, रईस दिल का इम्तिहान रखिये।

हानि एवं मुनाफे दोनों से अनुभव प्रप्त कीजिए,

ज़रूरत करने पर लागू कीजिए ।

- सहज सभरवाल

I ♡ MOM & DAD

आज का ज़माना ऐसे किस प्यार की तलाश में है, जिसके आगे उन्हें माँ-बाप का अनमोल प्रेम भी कम पड़ने लग गया है। जिन्होंने तुम्हें बनाया और बचपन से आज तक प्यार किया, तुम तो उस समय उन्हें ठीक से जानते भी नहीं थे। वे तुम्हें दिल से प्यार कल भी करेंगे, करते ही रहेंगे।

पर ना जाने क्यों तुम फिर भी किसी नए प्यार को पाने के लिए, असली प्यार को खोने को भी तैयार हो गए हो।

- सहज सभरवाल

" यह सच है कि आजकल भलाई का ज़माना नही है,

लेकिन फिर भी नेकी की राह पर चलते हुए, खुदगरज़ी के

नाम पर,

मानवता के भाव को डूबना नहीं है "

- सहज सभरवाल

एक उसके लिए मैने कितनों से मुँह मोड़ा है,

पर परवाह कहाँ इस मतलबी ज़माने मे उसे हमारी,

उसने तो एक असली शायर से मुँह मोड़ा है।

पहचान कर भी नज़र अंदाज कर उसने मेरा दिल चूर-चूर

कर तोड़ा है,

अहंकार नही है मुझमे, कोशिश पूरी थी मेरी।

अगर अब की बार भी उसने मुँह मोड़ा है,

तो समझ लेना कि शायर ने दिल से, जीवन भर के लिए

उसे छोड़ा है।

- सहज सभरवाल

हर पल साथ बिताना तो हर किसी का सपना होता है,

लेकिन जिंदगी में हर कोई थोड़ी ना अपना होता है।

खुदा ये परिवार के एक ही झूले मे रिश्तों का अटूट बंधन बनाकर झूलता ही है, अंदरूणी प्रेम का अर्थ सिखाने के लिए,

ताकि हर इंसान केवल जीवित रहना नहीं बल्कि जिंदगी को निःशंक मिलकर जिए।

- सहज सभरवाल

अपना क्या है ?

पहले बुरा कर्म करके तो जीवन भी सज़ा है,

अब तो ये जीवन ऐसा ही बीतेगा।

पर बिन हारे अच्छे कर्म करके तो,

अगले जन्म में तो मज़ा ही मज़ा है।

- सहज सभरवाल

STORIES

TALE OF MUNDU AND BAGDNI

Once upon a time, there was a girl named Bagdni and a boy named Mundu. Bagdini was studying in the same class as that of Mundu, a very much creative and clever boy. Just opposite to Mundu, Bagdni was a quite innocent and calm hearted girl. They both were best friends and used to play games with each other every day and study together always.

After three years, they both went out to study. But they both don't know that they will meet in the same college for study. They both were hardworking and helped each other a lot in study and assignment work. After a week of their starting their college, Mundu and Bagdni decided to go for a picnic in the nearby garden. They both were strangers there and don't know much regarding the place, but heard of it that it is a nice picnic spot but safe only while the day. They knew that at the night it's a very dangerous place as, during the night, the soul of the king used to harm people.

They heard a rumor that a foolish king was killed there by a small, clever brown mouse. The king, due to his ego, thought that no one can kill him, not even God and he was overconfident about that. So, the villagers who were tired of the orders of the king found a clever brown mouse which was the pet of a villager named Bampu. The 'clever' title was given to that brown mouse because he was very intelligent and told the king that he can't seek him and the foolish king tried to run after him to catch him. But the clever mouse jumped into a deep river. As that king don't know how to swim, he was not able to breathe as his nostrils were struck with water after ten minutes of the scene, the villagers arrived there and found that the king was dead. That mouse knew that that king doesn't have the knowledge to swim and the mouse was a very good swimming teacher. After that, as the wish of the king was not completed in his life to live a very long life and he didn't want to be killed by a small mouse at a very young age, his soul was whispering there only which harm people at the night.

Bagdni and Mundu after hearing this story from a person, started their journey towards that picnic spot by telling their driver that they have to reach there before 7 pm. But as they reached just two kilometers away, they stared their journey, suddenly their car driver observed a type of problem in the engine as the car was not moving properly and after some time, stopped automatically. And that area was also a forest area and there was no car mechanic nearby. The driver then tried to find the problem but was unable to make it work again. Both Mundu and Bagdni were waiting inside the car only, while the driver went for a walk to search for a mechanic.

By the time the driver returned, the time was around 5 pm, but fruitlessly, without any mechanic with him. Mundu, being a genius and intelligent science student, tried and succeeded in making the car engine work well by using the concepts he had studied seriously. The driver thanked and blessed Mundu for his creative mind and they started their journey ahead.

The time they reached the picnic spot, it was 7:30 pm, which was not the right time to have a visit to the garden of the venue. Being brave-hearted, the driver convinced both of them to have a visit there near the bright lighted area only. Bagdni and Mundu decided to have a meal in the restaurant nearby and then going there to have a walk there in the garden.

After having a nutritious dinner, they went to have a walk in the light sparkled area in the picnic spot.

While having a walk, Bagdni was first to start the walking track followed by Mundu followed by the driver. After five minutes of walk, Mundu noticed a type of strange noise in that calm, dark area. Bagdni was walking fast and reached six to seven meters far from Mundu, as observed by Mundu himself. Then, Mundu had a quick look backside to see the driver but was shocked to see no one behind him. Mundu was shocked and shouted "Driver Uncle". But his echo came back and no one else. Then he tried to run towards Bagdini by calling her. But she didn't stop. He thought that she was unable to hear him.

Then, he noticed a wild horse running sound but due to dark area was not able to see anything. Suddenly, he saw three men around him he was just like standing between a triangle as surrounded by the three men. Then, one of them tried to snatch the silver chain from his neck. He tried to save it and started shouting but he was unable to save his chain and no one around that spot, was able to hear him. Within five seconds of that, Mundu observed an attack from the backside with a rod and he fell.

He woke up in the midnight, around 11:45 pm and slowly got his senses back and observed that blood was coming out from his forehead and remembered about the scene which was happened with him. Then, his mind struck that Bagdni, his best friend was also with him and he anxiously started searching her. He found Bagdni in a prone position on a bench. She was just faint may be due to watching something strange and Mundu just, without considering his serious injury, was having attachment with her friend so that she could recover her consciousness. He was showing his seriousness and hospitality towards her. And after, Bagdni opened her eyes and Mundu felt relaxed and hugged her, showing his sympathy towards her.

Bagdini felt towards the injury on his forehead and gave her a scarf to him for covering the wound. They both consider the place to be unsafe at that time too. Then, Mundu called the police of that area and after that informed their parents regarding this. After a few minutes, the police came there and noted the details of the driver's car and found that the car driver was a registered criminal in their records.

The police took both of them to a safe place and called a doctor for treatment of Mundu's injury. The next day, one of the policemen found that criminal driver at the taxi stand and took him to jail and the Judge decided to give the criminal, life imprisonment considering his previous crimes.

The police inspector appreciated Mundu for calling the police at the right time.

Mundu and Bagdni thanked the police inspector for their great help and protection to them.

"Wake up my son, Its time to get ready for school," told my mother and I get to know that this is just my nightmare and I (Sahaj Sabharwal) get the plot for writing my story.

– Sahaj Sabharwal

BAMPU AND THE BEAR

Once upon a time, there was a young, 12 years old boy, named Bampu. He was fond of wild animals and used to visit a zoo twice a week. He loved all the animals and even took care of street dogs, cows, and buffaloes. His dream was to have a pet animal at his own home too. He was a pure vegan and avoided all animal products. He got a gift pet dog on his 13th Birthday from his parents. His happiness, excitement, and thankfulness had no limits. He took care of the dog just like caring for a newly born baby.

One day, when he was sleeping, a bear ran away from the zoo and came to the balcony of his home.

Suddenly, he woke up and went outside to see where the strange noise was coming from. He was shocked to see the bear and shouted loudly. As soon as his parents woke up and came outside, the bear held him in his hands, put him on his back and started running fast. At first, Bampu got afraid but after some time, he noticed that the bear was taking care of him. The bear took him to a jungle tour. Bampu was very much happy to have that enjoyable ride. When they reached the jungle, he saw thousands of animals gathered there at one particular place. The bear started introducing everyone in detail and told him the characteristics of all the animals. The boy shook hands with every animal and they told him that they had gathered solely to thank Bampu for his wonderful contribution to wildlife at that very young age and awarded him with the beautiful bracelet and a big basket of beautiful natural fruits. And then everyone stood up to give respect to their king, the Lion.

Lion also blessed him and appreciated him and told him to teach this valuable lesson to all the humans also. After the event, the boy enjoyed tasty meals there. After two days, Bampu told the bear that he wanted to go back home now because his parents would be worried about him. So, told every animal bade him goodbye! " The bear then took him back safely to his home and told him to take care as he bid farewell to him.

That was a wonderful experience for Bampu and he was so much motivated too. His parents were searching for him in the whole town and felt so much relaxed when they saw him back and then he told them the whole story of this adventure and requested his friends to "Save Wildlife".

Moral -: We must Save and take care of Wildlife

– Sahaj Sabharwal

ARTICLES

WHEN RESOURCES ARE SNATCHED, PEOPLE BECOME CRIMINALS

When the most valuable, as well as the necessary thing, is snatched from people,

Then people try to find out other ways of accessing that particular thing by any means. People at that intolerable state, get engaged in research for the alternatives to access it. The methods they try for accessing that desirable necessity includes crime and all illegal activities too.

For a live example, the Internet, which is the most desirable thing and without which most of the important works cannot be done and under that condition, Wi-Fi access is given to people as an alternative. When mobile network internet connection banned for some time due to some circumstances, in some areas of a country, People understand that there might be some important reasons for banning it. Some people who have a Wireless Fidelity connection can access it without any problem. But when common people are inaccessible to it, they show intolerable attitude, they cannot stop themselves from getting involved in doing crimes and illegal activities to access it.

Nowadays, there are many applications which are used to hack some Wi-Fi Illegally.

Actually, those applications are for the purpose of checking the security and vulnerability and used by people to crack Wps and Wpa Wi-Fi passwords and keys.

The use of those applications has been increasing day by day by the common people who want internet access without installing their own Wi-Fi at their home.

As these illegal applications are vulnerable, people find it so easy now to steal someone's Wi-Fi connection illegally.

These doings by people are big crimes.

Not only youth but also the old generation are accessing those illicit apps and want their work to be done free of cost and easily, which must not be done.

Either Government and concerned authorities should do something and find some more alternatives which are accessible by everyone who needs and if possible should settle the issue as soon as possible and making the conditions neutral.

– Sahaj Sabharwal

WHY WE CAN'T DISCERN GOD ?

Today is a world full of development in fields of Science and Technology by talented and artistic people . Different types of people live in this world. All of them, directly or indirectly have in build talents by creative God.

A few of them are atheistic while others are theistic. But all humans are the creation of almighty God. People worship God for their good and request God to keep them fit and healthy and to bless them . But they donot worship God with full concentration and attachment. Hindus worship their God in temples, Muslims worship their God in Mosques, Sikhs worship their God in Gurdwaras while Christians worship their God in Churches. But a very few people are able to find God. This is due to the concentration and love with God and full faith in God . Many people when go to their worship place , they keep on watching their surroundings and other people rather than God . They pay a very few time praying God. Some of them on sitting for long time in worship centre , get bored and to overcome it they use smartphones to chat , watch videos , play games , phone call their relatives , disturb others who are wholeheartedly worshiping God and conversate with other people around them . If they pay attention towards God and pray them honestly, they will definitely find God. Children in worship places try learn everything they watch around them and if adults do these things , this will have bad effect on young generation too . Children , if doing something wrong in worship centres is not their mistakes as they are immature but the mistake of their parents.

Parents are their future maker and must do best they can in front of them and in real life also as a child will follow characteristics of their parents only. While taking holy offerings (prasada) or blessings from the priests or food used as religious offerings the devotees often show their greed and want more quantity of blessings in form of ambrosia. This all is observed and noted as a record by God.

Not even the mistakes of devotees but the priests also do many mistakes in those religious places. Priest, now a days, are indulged in wrong activities . They show very less attention to the God and devotees and their concentration is on what a devotee offer to God and its quantity and priest show their greed and cleverness in it. Priests try to do brainwash of the devotees and this too is under the supervision of almighty God and provide the prasada/blessings depending on the quantity and quality of the thing or amount or money a person gives to the God . A priest must be an ideal ,good intelligent and calm hearted religious person who should never do any discrimination based on caste, creed, color or gender. A mind full of purity and good thoughts is necessary condition to find God. God never wants amount or quantity or quality of thing and not even the thing , but God only wants the wholehearted attention and attachment of the devotees to him. He wants nothing but the faith of a devotee and God is ready to give everything good, a devotee wants or wishes to get as God is the creator of this world. God always exists within the heart of everyone . If a pure mind of a noble person with full concentration, when tries to find God, just by closing eyes is guaranteed to get God's visit.

Moreover, now a days , people are keeping copy of pictures or God's statue at their homes. These pictures or statues are produced in bulk by the painters/artists or idolist/sculptor .

According to me ,this must not be done . As people produce various copies of God's pictures or statues and they are doing this just for their business. Except religious places, people are keeping the copy of God at their home, office , cars, using pictures of God in bracelets and necklaces . With this the value and purity of worship places are decreasing day by day . People carelessly keep God's pic anywhere and show very less respect to it . Many times , the industry where these sculpture or pictures are printed in bulk , they throw them in bundle or box from here to there and many of the prints tear off and statues are broken without considering them as a piece of worship and just try to gain maximum profits only by any means. But if on the same place , when God's statue is kept in a pure religious place, it will have considerable position and will be given great respect and faith. For example -: If a particular thing is present in large quantity, then people become unaware of it and they can use in whatever way they want and use it carelessly considering that if some quantity is used by a person then it will not affect the rest large quantity and waste it recklessly. On the other hand, if that particular this is present only in small amounts then people pay more attention to it and it become valuable for them and they take care of it very well considering that if people waste it they will not get if back easily again .

That's why for having great value of God's statues/pics, the quantity of copies must be less.

Moreover, in olden times people keep a lot of cleanliness and purity in God's home by keeping footwear far away from religious place but now it's not the same rule.

But people have now become very careless and pure less, as they keep their footwear in fact anywhere . Today is a time when people their self are making their own rules and keeping footwear wherever they want and even so near the worship place.

That's the reason why people are unable to find God and a few of calm hearted find God in today's world after a lot of true worship.

– Sahaj Sabharwal

COVID19

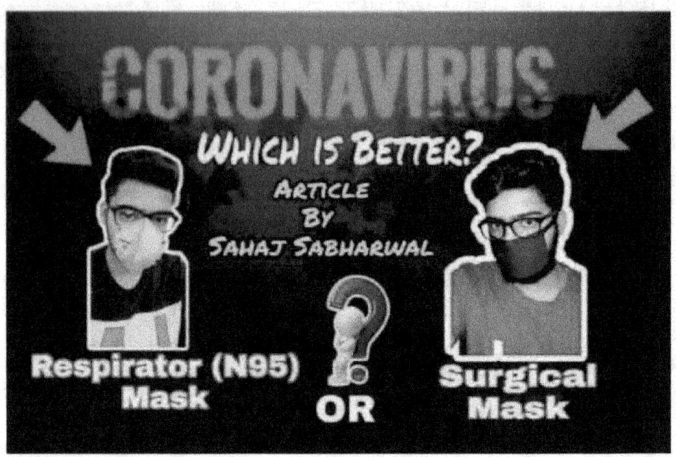

CAN SURGICAL MASKS OR RESPIRATORS PREVENT CORONA VIRUS ?

The world is suffering from the deadly infection of Coronavirus. The World Health Organization (WHO) has declared the infection as 'pandemic'. The early symptoms of this deadly infection are high fever, shortness of breath, tiredness and dry cough. So, the entire world is under lockdown to break the chain of COVID-19 with certain precautionary steps is to be ensured. The contemporary ways to sanitize oneself is the 20 seconds formulae of hand wash or using disinfectant containing at least 60% alcohol, avoid touching surfaces and handshakes and no unnecessary contacts. The use of mask and covering face using napkin or elbow while coughing and disposing the napkin would add an added advantage.

We all know that sanitizer containing good quality alcohol can kill most of the germs, bacteria and viruses including fatal Coronavirus . In a research, it was found that the Coronavirus can survive for 3 days (72 hours approx.) On surfaces like steel or plastic.

Now , the question arises whether any face masks or covering mouth with any cloth helps to prevent Coronavirus from invading our body ?

Firstly, I want to let you know that no mask can provide 100% safety from Corona Virus. There are different types of masks available in market and most common of them are Surgical masks and Respirators.

They act as a barrier to prevent the foreign body from entering our body, but the main difference between them is that Surgical masks are used only to prevent dust particles or large particle droplets that enter through our nose or mouth while Respirators can prevent vapours, airborne microorganisms, fumes or particulate matter that enter through nose or mouth . But as we know that the virus can enter our body through eyes so the person wearing a spectacles or googles can help prevent Covid19 to enter body to some extent . As spectacles or googles are left open from its sides so virus can reach our eyes easily. Hence, it is advised to stay at home and take precautionary steps while stepping out of home. The frontline workers including police, media persons, essential service and sweepers wear face shield along with N95 masks to safeguard themselves.

Surgical masks are mostly used by people who are not into any essential services as these are not designed to protect the wearer from breathing in airborne bacteria or viruses. Coronavirus is smaller than the PM 2.5 cutoff but bigger than some regular dust particles and gases. These masks can be used by a person with weak immune system or suffering from chronic health diseases. Persons dealing with severe respiratory or breathing issues are more prone to get infected from coronavirus, hence it is advisable for the infected person to use face mask as well in order to protect others from getting infected. The use of masks is also recommended to healthy person from getting infected. Surgical masks are of three types-: 2-layered surgical mask , 3-layered surgical mask and 6-layered surgical mask

The protection also depends on the number of layer, more number of layers contribute more protection. A 3-layered mask is better than 2-layered masks, the cost of 3-layered mask is also higher than 2-layered mask. While the 6-layered masks are best till now as it can protect us from some of the viruses but cannot protect from SARS cov-2 to enter the body This type of mask is loose-fitting and virus can easily enter through the opening sides. And one more drawback is that it is not having any particular side from which a person have to wear it. So as a human it's common to make mistake and use different side to wear while reusing, keeping it anywhere after using can spread risk of virus at that particular place and without knowledge of its proper way of wearing help the virus to enter the body. Also, the outer layer of the mask consists of virus and accidental touching can lead to the novel coronavirus.

As mostly surgical masks tend to be disposable, it get wet due to water vapours generated during respiration, that means they need to be replaced with new mask or washable 6-layered mask, washing it with 60°C hot water with a disinfectant to kill the germs can help in reusing them.

Respirators are used by health professionals as they are having contact with infected person quite often. These are at a risk of getting contaminated by infected person that's why they use it along with face shield to be more secure from the Coronavirus. N95 mask is most common respirator consisting of filters that can prevent 95% i.e 0.3 micron airborne particles. It is a type of mechanical filter respirator and is better than any type of surgical mask. Respirator is tight fitting and have no opening , it protects in a better way. It protects us from most of the viruses which enter from mouth or nose openings but still protects against SARS cov-2 to small extent. When someone around us coughs or sneezes then the germs or droplets exhaled can stick on a person's clothes or long hair especially in women, so the hair must be covered with a cloth while going out and changing clothes after coming back to home is recommended. For men too keeping a long bushy beard and facial hair are also prone to Corona virus so best way is to avoid going out or to keep short or no beard on face or clean it after every outside tour. It contains valve which releases unfiltered air when the wearer breathes out, hence the spread cannot be stopped just by using respirator.

So along with respirator, using a sanitizer is must, to clean our hands from time to time. A respirator cannot be reused and after a particular time period of usage it becomes difficult for us to breath through it and it indicates the time to replace or dispose after use. Most of the doctors and nurses who are curing the Corona patients use surgical masks, face shield, Personal Protective Equipments (PPE) kits and respirator to get best protection. No doubt, for full day wearing cause skin irritation and problems especially in the summer season, discomfort due to sweat on the human body, but still to save life and to contribute the nation, the Corona Warriors are doing their best work to keep us safe during this crucial period.

Therefore, for the common people, the best way is isolation and social distancing. Mask is better than no mask. A common man must keep physical distance from everyone and use sanitizers to kill the microorganisms on hands and wrist. In fact, if we apply some sanitizer over the mask before using then the germs which stick will be killed at the moment and the mask will be more risk free. And if a person is having any symptoms of COVID-19, then he much contact the health care team or can go to a hospital for checkup. As prevention is better than cure, all things must be kept in mind to fight this virus. If tested positive than he can get cured. Either the person has good immunity or should intake healthy foods for boosting immune system, for example, Citrus fruits, broccoli, garlic, ginger, spinach, curd and almonds are best immunity boosters, drinking plenty of normal water everyday also help in keeping our body fit. Immunity system helps in recovery.

If we, common people maintain social distancing and use just any cloth mask or scarf or just simple 3-layered or 6-layered, it is enough with respect to follow all precautionary measures then there will be no problem as such balefully.

That's why Stay Home, Stay Safe, Stay Healthy & Stay Fit and the world will soon defeat this Coronavirus.

– Sahaj Sabharwal

SC/OBC/ST ARE VIP CATEGORIES IN MODERN COMPETITION OVER GENERAL

Race in the modern world is a phase, from which no one can chase.

Today's world runs after competition and every single contestant runs with the aim to win in it. But unfortunately, everybody can't win it, but everyone aims and will be glad to win. Due to a few vacancies available at the winning position, many have to return home to practice again and to try again the next time.

Out of those who returns home, only a few of them get motivated, having a positive mindset, learns with the loss

While the others feel demotivated and think that its failure for them in life.

But actually its not a failure, everyone who participated, practiced well and aimed to win is a winner. Because the winner is just because of luck and a little more efforts. The winners' positions are less that's why it is never a fair competition and not a genuine way to check the power, talent or skills of a particular contestant.

In our world, in a pen paper or online exams, someone can pass with pass by unauthorized tricks such as cheating, corruption, nepotism etc. And after the results of that particular exam, if a particular cheater wins, then he/she will be determined as a winner without any verification or something, whether that person has some good skills or not. That's why, just an examination is never the best way to to check inner talents and exceptional skills.

In India, Scheduled Castes (SCs), Scheduled Tribes (STs) and Other Backward Classes (OBCs) are officially designated people's groups.

According to SC/ST act (1989),

Parliament of India enacted to prohibit discrimination , prevent atrocities and hate crimes against the scheduled castes and the scheduled tribes.

Other Backward Class (OBC) is a collective term used by the Government of India to classify castes which are educationally or socially disadvantaged.

In the earlier times, those who deserves to be given special rights and reservations, were really worthy as general or higher class people were creating hate crimes, untouchability, discriminations based on caste etc.

So, in order to provide equal status to them just like general categories, laws were introduced. Moreover, SC, ST & OBC were economically backward classes so the Government of India introduced some special laws especially for them just to cope up with their problems and stand alike in race with the general category. The special laws includes some reserved seats for them in mostly every field.

But nowadays, SC/ST/OBC are on a better position than before even better than those of general category.

They are utilizing their special reservations in the perfect way.

In fact, they have grown to that much standards that they are leaving back the general category.

Many of the general category people, sitting idle, being unemployed because of lack of jobs and opportunities. As the special VIP treatment i.e reservations even for jobs and opportunities, whether they have that potential/quality or not, quota has been fixed for the SC,ST & OBC. Due to this, many of the general category aspirants, even if they have that talent and quality to get the job/opportunity have to suffer. Because the opportunities are less for them.

As earlier discussed, in the past, being undeveloped or not of that standard, this special reservation quota was given to the lower classes, but now, most of them are well developed and they are becoming more rich/capable as compared to the general class. So, these reservations and all should be given to those who really need them. There are many people in general category too who deserve to get a respectable/higher position due to their potential but not given because these special reservations are only for the lower classes by name, in actual they are higher, nowadays. Lower category is now a tag/brand that if you are in it, you will be given VIP rights even if you don't deserve. Laws must be made to give the special reservations to praiseworthy people, those who actually deserve, those who don't have money, but merit, those who are actually illiterate, but are poor to afford education costs or those who are talented/unique to help them rise.

According to Sahaj Sabharwal,

A brand/tag without a quality,

Is like a truth without a reality.

Provide to those who deserve and serve,

Not those who just eat someone's position and their wrong phase they shamelessly observe.

– Sahaj Sabharwal

THANK YOU!

Once again, a very big thank you to the Almighty for making this happen. For showing me my real potential at the right time with a fruitful set of experiences.

Thank you, my dear readers, for supporting this work of mine by reading my writings.

Dear Mate,
Please don't hate,
If you can't relate.

Do forgive me for my mistakes. I have simply shared my original views as a real writer.

"A writer is a great mind fighter, having a pen full of heavy thoughts, but still lighter."

This book was one of my virtual dreams which is now a real truth. All that I penned down is purely unedited.

"Pedagogical Thoughts Made Facts."

Hope you all enjoyed reading my work. Looking ahead to provide you more of such works to motivate you and become your inspiration with much more love. Keep supporting and improving me.

I write & fight

Because my 🖋 pen isn't tight. 

www.ingramcontent.com/pod-product-compliance
Lightning Source LLC
LaVergne TN
LVHW041312200726
843509LV00009B/467